Anonymous Christians

Anonymous Christians

Support by Clergy of Addiction Recovery
through Twelve Step Programs

Herbert E. Hudson IV

Foreword by Robert H. Albers

RESOURCE *Publications* • Eugene, Oregon

ANONYMOUS CHRISTIANS
Support by Clergy of Addiction Recovery through Twelve Step Programs

Copyright © 2017 Herbert E. Hudson IV. All rights reserved. Except for brief quotations in critical publications or reviews, no part of this book may be reproduced in any manner without prior written permission from the publisher. Write: Permissions, Wipf and Stock Publishers, 199 W. 8th Ave., Suite 3, Eugene, OR 97401.

Resource Publications
An Imprint of Wipf and Stock Publishers
199 W. 8th Ave., Suite 3
Eugene, OR 97401

www.wipfandstock.com

PAPERBACK ISBN: 978-1-5326-3457-4
HARDCOVER ISBN: 978-1-5326-3459-8
EBOOK ISBN: 978-1-5326-3458-1

Manufactured in the U.S.A.   NOVEMBER 30, 2018

The Twelve Steps and brief excerpts from the Twelve Steps and Twelve Traditions are reprinted with permission of Alcoholics Anonymous World Services, Inc. ("A.A.W.S.") Permission to reprint this material does not mean that A.A.W.S. has reviewed or approved the contents of this publication, or that A.A.W.S. necessarily agrees with the views expressed herein. A.A. is a program of recovery from alcoholism only-use of the Twelve Steps in connection with programs and activities which are patterned after A.A., but which address other problems, or in any other non-A.A. context, does not imply otherwise. Additionally, while A.A. is a spiritual program, A.A. is not a religious program. Thus, A.A. is not affiliated or allied with any sect, denomination, or specific religious belief.

Celebrate Recovery's 12 Steps and Biblical Comparisons and Eight Recovery Principles are reprinted from their website with permission of Celebrate Recovery.

All Scripture quotations, unless otherwise indicated, are taken from the Holy Bible, New International Version®, NIV®. Copyright ©1973, 1978, 1984, 2011 by Biblica, Inc.™ Used by permission of Zondervan. All rights reserved worldwide. www.zondervan.com The "NIV" and "New International Version" are trademarks registered in the United States Patent and Trademark Office by Biblica, Inc.™

To my grandchildren
Adam, Danielle, Samantha, Leah, Kyle, and Matthew
My children Deborah, Wendy, and Sean
And my love, Teresa

Contents

List of Illustrations | *x*

List of Tables | *xi*

Foreword by Robert H. Albers | *xiii*

Acknowledgments | *xv*

Chapter 1.   Introduction | 1

    Culture and the Significance of Addiction
    Interventions
    Relationship of the Topic to the Ministry of the Writer
    Scope and Limitations
    Goals and Objectives

Chapter 2.   Theological and Biblical Perspectives | 19

    Humanity: Sin and Disease
    God: Omnipotence, Abundance, and Forgiveness
    Christ: Prophet of Healing
    Prayer: Between Humanity and God
    Miracles: Between God and Humanity
    Koinonia: Empowerment of Fellowship
    Summary

Chapter 3.   Issues from Related Contemporary Literature | 37

    Literature on Knowledge Deficits in Addictionology
    Literature on History and Background of Twelve Step Programs

CONTENTS

    Literature Explaining How Twelve Step Organizations Work
    Literature on the Spiritual Features of the Twelve Step Design and Its Relation to Christianity
    Literature on Current Information on Addiction Theory
    Literature on the General Subject of Addiction Treatment
    Summary

Chapter 4.   Narrative of Research Execution | 81

    Methodology
    Research Execution
    Replicating the Research
    Observation on the Pastorate and Summary

Chapter 5.   Research Evaluation | 87

    First Goal: Understanding Pre-conditions of Pastors' Views
    Second Goal: Ascertaining How Informed Pastors Are on Addiction and the Twelve Step Format
    Third Goal: Determining Attitudes of Clergy Toward the Twelve Step Model
    Fourth Goal: How Research Informs the Outcome of a Course Syllabus for Training Clergy
    A General Narrative of What Pastors Shared
    Summary

Chapter 6.   Development of a Syllabus | 111

    Survey of Existing Courses
    The Syllabus for a Course
    Summary

Chapter 7.   Conclusion | 117

    Lessons Learned
    Afterword

Appendix A. Behavioral Manifestations and Complications of Addiction | 125

Appendix B. Alcohol Use Disorder Diagnostic Criteria | 126

Appendix C. Gambling Disorder Diagnostic Criteria | 128

Appendix D. Questionnaire Including Statement of Informed Consent | *129*

Appendix E. Informed Consent Statement for Interview | *134*

Appendix F. Interview Questions | *135*

Appendix G. Outline of the Syllabus | *137*

Bibliography | *141*

List of Illustrations

Figure 1. Original A.A. Steps by Bill Wilson | 7

Figure 2. PowerPoint slides for "Resilience in Addiction Recovery Symposium" | 75

Figure 3. Age of Pastors | 89

Figure 4. Attended a Twelve Step Meeting | 95

Figure 5. Addiction a Disease, Not a Sin | 102

Figure 6. Twelve Steps Based Upon Christianity | 104

List of Tables

Table 1. History of Addiction in Families of Pastors | 88

Table 2. Age of Pastors | 89

Table 3. Gender of Pastors | 90

Table 4. Denomination of Pastors | 90

Table 5. Responses of Pastors Not from Mainline Protestant Churches | 91

Table 6. Education of Pastors | 91

Table 7. How Knowledgeable Pastors Are on Addiction | 93

Table 8. Florida Keys Susceptible to Addiction | 93

Table 9. How Familiar Pastors Are with Twelve Step Format | 94

Table 10. How Familiar Pastors Are with Christ-Centered Twelve Step Programs | 96

Table 11. Perceptions of Pastors about Church Members with Addictions | 96

Table 12. How Favorable Pastors Are Toward Twelve Step Programs | 98

Table 13. Attitude of Pastors Toward Those in Recovery from Addiction | 99

Table 14. Outcomes of Pastors' Support of Twelve Step Groups | 100

Table 15. Addiction a Disease, Not a Sin | 101

Table 16. Twelve Steps Based Upon Christianity | 103

Table 17. Attitude of Pastors toward Christ-Centered Programs | 105

Foreword

THIS WELL-WRITTEN VOLUME SPAWNED by the concern and convictions of an author who is dedicated to ministry with those afflicted by addiction, and also those adversely affected by addiction, constitutes an important contribution to the literature in this field.

The exhaustive delving into the history of addiction and recovery contributes critically important insights regarding the evolution of the recovery process. The author is honest and intentional about his own desire to provide a proposed syllabus for clergy who are Christian, in terms of their theological commitments that inform their ministry.

As a consequence, he provides his interpretation of salient biblical texts that inform his angle of vision about the topic of addiction and recovery. His focus on the centrality of the community as the healing agent for addiction is congruent with his objective in this study. He delves deeply into the theological implications and conclusions reached by significant others in the field who have devoted substantive time and thought to these critical concerns.

His research and writing is precise and meticulous in attaining his stated objective. It is noteworthy that he includes disparate voices in articulating what addiction and recovery represent to those who are engaged in ministry from a Christian perspective. Consequently, one of the intentions of his research was to focus on both the personal experience as well as the theological convictions of the clergy interviewed in his study. It brings to light a very critical hermeneutical issue, as to the way clergy do theology and ministry. Is a theological tradition the primary factor in forming an attitude about addiction, or is the personal experience of the clergyperson and her or his ministry most integral in contributing to an evolving theology? The

Foreword

hermeneutical circle can be completed only when both a theological tradition and the impact of experience are given equal salience.

His chosen research methodology informs the reader where clergy are located as he utilizes a "mixed method" of research involving both the quantitative and qualitative forms in gathering the data for his work. The questionnaire, as well as the personal interviews, result in creating a detailed picture of the clergy, and their attitudes and actions, in relationship to addiction and recovery in this selected geographical location of the Florida Keys.

The consequence of this carefully designed research project is to extrapolate from what was learned, to create a syllabus that takes into consideration the history and the scientific research done on addiction and recovery, as well as the theological framework articulated from a Christian perspective. The author does an excellent job of defining his intent and purpose and providing data from his research to make a strong case for educating clergy who are on the front lines of this battle with one of the nation's most devastating problems.

This book will find eager readers among those who are dedicated to addressing this pervasive phenomenon in the context of their communities of faith.

Robert H. Albers
Distinguished Visiting Professor of Pastoral Care at United Theological Seminary of the Twin Cities

Acknowledgments

THIS BOOK IS BASED upon a dissertation at Trinity Evangelical and Divinity School titled, "Development of a Syllabus for Pastors and Those in Ministerial Training on Addiction Recovery Through Twelve Step Philosophy" (Hudson 2016a). I owe a debt of gratitude to my advisor, Martin R. Crain, and to members of my doctoral committee, Julie West Russo, James R. Moore, and William P. Donahue. In addition, I am deeply appreciative to Florida Keys ministerial association leaders Phillip A. Underwood and Randolph W. B. Becker, and the many pastors of the Florida Keys who contributed to this research. I am indebted to Robert H. Albers for his encouragement and for writing the foreword. Special thanks go to Maria Teresa Kwalick and Evelio Enrique Astray-Caneda III for editorial support. Finally, I am grateful to Matthew Wimer and his associates at Wipf and Stock Publishers, whose expertise and thoroughness helped make this book a reality.

Chapter 1

Introduction

"But God chose the foolish things of the world to shame the wise;
God chose the weak things of the world to shame the strong."
—1 Cor 1:27 [All biblical citations are from NIV,
unless otherwise noted]

THE FIRST RECORDED ABUSE of alcohol was by Noah, shortly after the Great Flood (Gen 9:20–23). Noah planted a vineyard and discovered the secret of wine-making. As is true of addiction, he was not content with simply tasting the wine and drinking in moderation. He apparently liked its effect and drank to excess, becoming drunk and passing out inside his tent where he lay naked. Moreover, Noah's drunkenness deeply affected other family members. His son, Ham, found him and went outside and told his two brothers what he had seen. Displaying behavior typical of co-dependency, his brothers, Shem and Japheth, walked into the tent backward so they would not see their father unclothed, and laid a garment over him. The negative effect of excessive drinking on Noah's family was immediately evident. When he awoke, doubtless with a hangover and learned what had happened, Noah flew into a rage against Ham, who had first come upon him and saw him naked. There were also transgenerational effects of Noah's drunkenness. According to Scripture, he cursed Ham and his offspring, Canaan, declaring they would be the slaves of Shem and his descendants, the people of Israel.[1]

---

1. Some theologians also interpret this passage as a reproof against same-sex relations. Genesis reads, "When Noah awoke from his wine and found out what his youngest

CULTURE AND THE SIGNIFICANCE OF ADDICTION

Our postmodern culture populated by Boomers, Gen Xers, and now by Gen Yers, has been variously described as relativistic and narcissistic (Ryken 2003, 18). "Superficiality is the curse of our age," observes Richard J. Foster, "The doctrine of instant satisfaction is a primary spiritual problem" (Foster 2008, 1). Patrick J. Carnes, a seminal author on sex addiction, asserts that we have an "addictive culture" that is *"convenience-oriented,"* has *"sophisticated technology,"* pursues *"entertainment and escapism,"* and has been "experiencing massive *paradigm shifts*" (Carnes 1991, 75–76; italics his).

The use of alcohol and other drugs has increased to the point where addiction is arguably our nation's number one public health problem (Schneider Institute for Health Policy 2001, accessed April 2015). David Sheff refers to this in the title of his book as *America's Greatest Tragedy* (Sheff 2013). The financial cost of drug abuse in the United States alone is more than four hundred billion dollars a year in lost productivity, crime, and health expenses (Sheff 2013, xvii). In the 1980s, Ronald Reagan declared war on addiction and made law enforcement a priority. Of course, it was not addiction or drugs that were punished, but people. The war on drugs became, in effect, a war on the American people. The result is that we have now incarcerated two million four hundred thousand citizens, four times the number in prison in 1980. "85 percent of the U.S. jail and prison population is incarcerated because of crimes committed on or related to drugs" (Sheff 2013, 285). We have the highest incidence of imprisonment of any nation; Russia is in a distant second place. William L. White concludes: "The late twentieth century witnessed the wholesale movement of people with alcohol and other drug problems—particularly poor people of color—from treatment programs to the criminal justice system" (White 2014, 526). This mass incarceration is so serious that another writer has termed it "The New Jim Crow" (Alexander 2012, 178).

---

son had done to him" (Gen 9:24). The implication is that what Ham "had done" was more than seeing his father naked; it may, in fact, have been homosexual rape (Gagnon 2001, 63–71).

INTRODUCTION

INTERVENTIONS

Intervention on addiction in America dates to Benjamin Rush in the late eighteenth century. He was a signer of the Declaration of Independence, Physician-General of the Continental Army, and a prolific writer. According to White, "No one writing on the subject of alcohol was more influential in early American history than Dr. Benjamin Rush" (White 2014, 2). Rush described the effects of excessive drinking and advocated abstinence from distilled alcohol in his unprecedented tract, *An Inquiry into the Effects of Ardent Spirits Upon the Human Body and Mind* (Rush 2011). Since then, organized interventions have included the Temperance Movement, the Washingtonians, the Emmanuel Movement, the Oxford Group, and most recently Alcoholics Anonymous.

Temperance Movement

The Temperance Movement began in the early 1800s to substitute moderate for excessive drinking, as its name implies. White acknowledges, "a shift from this view of temperance-as-moderation to temperance-as-abstinence unfolded between 1800 and 1825" (White 2014, 6). The American Temperance Society originated in 1826, and the Women's Christian Temperance Union started shortly after the Civil War. Americans of Anglo-Saxon heritage and Puritan tradition had begun associating alcohol abuse with the growing number of Catholic immigrants from Ireland and Europe. The Social Gospel element of evangelical Protestantism inspired the movement, which included Methodists, Presbyterians, Baptists, Congregationalists, Society of Friends, Universalists, Seventh Day Adventists, and Latter Day Saints. One of Temperance's most colorful supporters, Carrie Nation, stormed barrooms and smashed whiskey bottles and furniture with her iconic hatchet. Two commentators remark on the significance of the Temperance Movement:

> Temperance and related religious social movements produced social tributaries that permanently shaped the landscape of addiction recovery, treatment, and prevention programs in the United States. . . . Among the most important of these tributaries are spiritual and religious mutual help organizations. (Humphreys and Gifford 2006, 257)

The Temperance Movement created a cultural climate for addressing alcoholism and helping the alcoholic. "It was the failure of the temperance movement [however] that accounts for the emergence of A.A." (Woolverton 1983, 157, accessed December 2015).

Washingtonian Society

The Washingtonian Total Abstinence Society of the mid-1800s was a short-lived but remarkable phenomenon. Abraham Lincoln, a lifetime abstainer, appeared as a speaker before the Springfield Washingtonians on February 22, 1842. He said in part, "In my judgment such of us who have never fallen victims [of alcoholism], have been spared more by the absence of appetite than from any mental or moral superiority over those who have" (White 2014, 15). As one historian declares, "It was the first widely available mass mutual-aid society organized by and for alcoholics in American history" (White 2014, 20). Katherine McCarthy elaborates:

> The ideas of self-help and mutual support as alcoholism treatment were not original to the Emmanuel Movement [or A.A.]. The best-known historical antecedent was the Washingtonian Movement of the 1840s, a large group of abstinent alcoholics and nonalcoholic temperance advocates who achieved brief but spectacular success at "reforming" drunkards. (McCarthy 1984, 64)

The Washingtonians found that small groups enhanced personal recovery, but that relapse of publically known leaders could be harmful to the organization as a whole. Thus, Alcoholics Anonymous learned to place a premium on anonymity. A.A.'s Eleventh Tradition states, "We need always maintain personal anonymity at the level of press, radio, and films" (Alcoholics Anonymous World Services 2011, 180). Clearly, the Washingtonian Movement "laid a foundation of experience that guided alcoholism mutual-aid movements that followed" (White 2014, 20). The group was unsuccessful because of a multiplicity of causes, including failure to encourage the role of churches (White 2014, 19). They felt their fellowship alone was sufficient and that a spiritual component would be a turn-off for drunks. The group also failed because it became embroiled in political controversies, such as the abolition of slavery. Alcoholics Anonymous learned not to become involved in outside issues. A.A.'s Tenth Tradition affirms, "Alcoholics Anonymous has no opinion on outside issues; hence the A.A. name ought never be drawn into public controversy" (Alcoholics Anonymous World Services 2011, 176).

INTRODUCTION

Emmanuel Movement and the Jacoby Club

Rev. Elwood Worcester founded the Emmanuel Movement in 1906 at the Emmanuel Episcopal Church in Boston, and its offshoot, the Jacoby Club, began in 1909. With ties to the medical establishments of Harvard and Boston, the Emmanuel Movement integrated spirituality, basic psychological treatment, and "the idea and practice of fellowship as a path to recovery" (Dubiel 2004, xi). Richard M. Dubiel points out, "There is little doubt that the contributions of the Emmanuel Movement were significant in terms of the formulation of Alcoholics Anonymous" (Dubiel 2004, 33). Courtenay Baylor, a lay therapist, began working with Worcester in 1912 in a clinic at the Emmanuel Church. One of Baylor's protégés was Richard R. Peabody, who published *Common Sense of Drinking* in 1930, a book that would prove to be source material for the writing of the basic text of A.A. in 1938 and 1939. Peabody offered hope that alcoholism was treatable, as McCarthy indicates, "The major significance of Peabody's work was probably not its long-term therapeutic success but the hope that it gave, both to researchers in the early scientific study of alcoholism and to early A.A. members, that alcoholism was a treatable condition" (McCarthy 1984, 72). Even more strategically, Baylor provided counseling to Rowland Hazard, who later helped recruit Ebby Thatcher to the Oxford Group. Thatcher was destined to carry the message of recovery to William Griffith Wilson, co-founder of Alcoholics Anonymous.

The Oxford Group

In the early twentieth century, various parachurch structures were formed as a result of "an evangelical movement known as pietism" (Van Gelder 2000, 61). Personal experience with God became the emphasis, and the church assumed a secondary role. One such structure was the Oxford Group founded by Lutheran pietist, Frank Buchman. The Oxford Group is not to be confused with the Oxford Movement, which was a phenomenon of the nineteenth-century Anglican Church promoting High-Church practice. A.A. historian Ernest Kurtz points out, "The Oxford Group, out of which Alcoholics Anonymous sprang, shared deeply in the Evangelical Pietist insight" (Kurtz 1991, 179). Buchman was an ordained Lutheran minister who worked in a hospice for children, but he resigned following a budget dispute with his board of directors. Filled with resentment, he traveled to England and had a spiritual experience that both convicted him of his self-centeredness and led him to ask for forgiveness and make restitution to the members of the board. He decided to share this experience with others, and his efforts resulted in the formation of the Oxford Group.

Kurtz describes the Oxford Group as a "non-denominational, theologically conservative, evangelically styled attempt to recapture the impetus and spirit of what its members understood to be primitive Christianity" (Kurtz 1991, 9). It did not so much attract the disadvantaged or marginalized, but appealed to the prosperous and socially accepted, including such notables as Harry Truman, Joe DiMaggio and Henry Ford. Partly in reaction to the Social Gospel Movement, which applied Christian ethics to social problems, the Oxford Group "located the entire problem of human existence in personal sinfulness, the entire solution in individual conviction, confession, and surrender" (Mercadante 1996a, 51). In addition to having an impact in the United States, the Oxford Group became an international organization. When Buchman endorsed Hitler at the beginning of World War II, the Oxford Group fell out of favor and attempted to shake the negative publicity by changing its name to Moral Re-Armament.

A.A. Rooted in the Emmanuel Movement and the Oxford Group

The Emmanuel Movement was Christian and strongly psychological in emphasis, stressing the treatability of alcoholism, the importance of total abstinence, and group support. It utilized both individual and group therapy, sharing of personal experience, relaxation therapy, and the power of suggestion. The Oxford Group stressed Bible study and changing the world by personal responsibility. It emphasized belief in God and prayer, personal honesty and confession to others, restitution for wrongs done, small group accountability, and service to others.

Therefore, Alcoholics Anonymous was Christian in origin, having its roots in both the Emmanuel Movement and the Oxford Group. A.A. relied upon theoretical and treatment principles of the Emmanuel Movement, and directly converted the six principles of the Oxford Group into what became the Twelve Steps. (For a photocopy of the six principles written in Bill Wilson's own hand, possibly for Fr. Ed Dowling, SJ, see Figure 1.) The six precepts that came from the Oxford Group were as follows:

Introduction

1. We admitted we were powerless over alcohol.
2. We got honest with ourselves.
3. We got honest with another person, in confidence.
4. We made amends for harms done others.
5. We worked with other alcoholics without demand for prestige or money.
6. We prayed to God to help us to do these things as best we could (White 2014, 176; italics his).

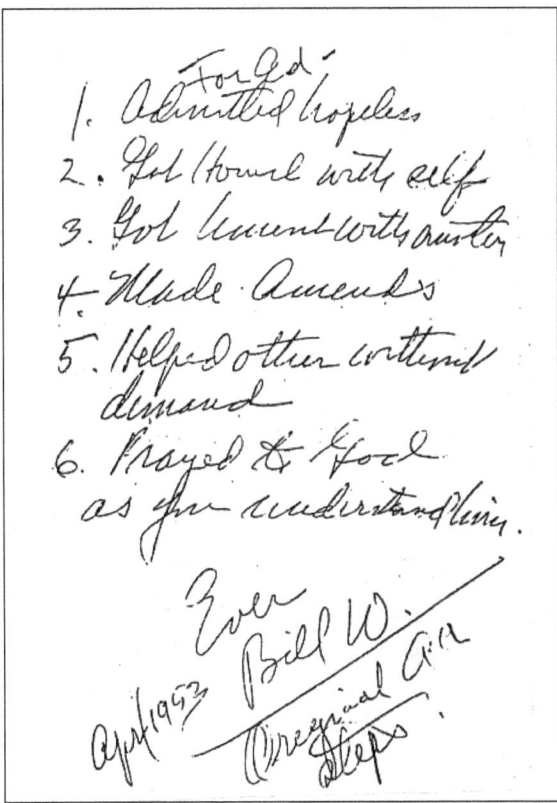

Figure 1: Original A.A. Steps by Bill Wilson (Wilson 1953, accessed September 2016). A copy of this document is in the archives of the General Service Office of Alcoholics Anonymous in New York.

These six principles from the Oxford Group were converted into the Twelve Steps of Alcoholics Anonymous:

1. We admitted we were powerless over alcohol—that our lives had become unmanageable.
2. Came to believe that a Power greater than ourselves could restore us to sanity.
3. Made a decision to turn our will and our lives over to the care of God *as we understood Him.*
4. Made a searching and fearless moral inventory of ourselves.
5. Admitted to God, to ourselves, and to another human being the exact nature of our wrongs.
6. Were entirely ready to have God remove all these defects of character.
7. Humbly asked Him to remove our shortcomings.
8. Made a list of all persons we had harmed, and became willing to make amends to them all.
9. Made direct amends to such people wherever possible, except when to do so would injure them or others.
10. Continued to take personal inventory and when we were wrong promptly admitted it.
11. Sought through prayer and meditation to improve our conscious contact with God *as we understood Him,* praying only for knowledge of His will for us and the power to carry that out.
12. Having had a spiritual awakening as the result of these steps, we tried to carry this message to alcoholics, and to practice these principles in all our affairs. (Alcoholics Anonymous World Services 1955, 59–60; italics theirs. Reprinted with permission of Alcoholics Anonymous World Services, Inc.)

Linda A. Mercadante concludes, "the Oxford Group heritage continues to deeply inform the program, principles and practices of AA [sic]" (Mercadante 2009, 99).

The co-founders of A.A., Bill Wilson and Dr. Bob Smith, had robust Christian backgrounds, and were both active in the Oxford Group. Bill was from East Dorset, New Hampshire, and his paternal grandparents were founders and officials of the East Dorset Congregational Church.

Introduction

He attended Sunday School and became involved in revivals, conversion, and Temperance meetings. He went to Burr and Burton Academy, which required daily chapel and weekly church attendance, where he took a four-year Bible study course, and became president of the Young Men's Christian Association. At the height of his drinking, "around December 7, 1934, Bill went to Calvary Mission, accepted Jesus Christ as his Lord and Savior, [and] later wrote that he had been born again" (Dick B. and Ken B. 2012, 62). To broaden his spiritual base, Bill received several years of religious instruction from Bishop Fulton J. Sheen. Two of his closest friends and confidants were Rev. Samuel M. Shoemaker, acknowledged leader of the Oxford Group in the United States, and Fr. Ed Dowling, SJ, of St. Louis, who was his non-alcoholic sponsor and who he characterized as "one of A.A.'s greatest friends" (Alcoholics Anonymous World Services 2011, 63). As Bill testifies, "The spiritual substance of our remaining ten Steps came straight from Dr. Bob's and my own earlier association with the Oxford Groups, as they were then led in America by that Episcopal rector, Dr. Samuel Shoemaker" (Wilson 2011, 298). Wilson explains his reason for breaking from the Oxford Group, "The Oxford Group wanted to save the world, and I only wanted to save drunks" (White 2014, 174).

Dr. Bob was raised in the North Congregational Church in St. Johnsbury, Vermont, one of the churches impacted by Christian Endeavor Society evangelism. His father taught Sunday School for forty years, and "Bob was soaked in conversion meetings, prayer meetings, Bible study, Quiet Hours, Christian fellowship, confessions of Christ, and Christian love and service. . . . he himself never lost his status as a born-again child of God" (Dick B. 2005, 162). He continued being active in church throughout his life and regularly took his children to Sunday School. In Bill's last major talk, he reminisced about Dr. Bob: "I remember how perfectly Bob put it to them. He reminded us that most of us were practicing Christians. Then he asked, 'What would the Master have thought?'" (Alcoholics Anonymous World Services 1975a, 30). If someone asked Bob "a question about the program, his usual response was: 'What does it say in the Good Book [the Bible]?'" (Alcoholics Anonymous World Services 1980, 144). When Dr. Bob stopped drinking, people asked him what his "non-drinking" group was. "'A Christian fellowship,' he'd reply" (Alcoholics Anonymous World Services 1980, 118). In an early attempt to stop or at least moderate his drinking, Dr. Bob became active in the Oxford Group in Akron, Ohio. His Oxford Group acquaintance, Henrietta Seiberling, was responsible for introducing him to Bill Wilson in May 1935.

Alcoholics Anonymous

Wilson got sober in December 1934, a year in religious history that has been termed *annus mirabilis,* or "wondrous year," ushering in the age of neo-orthodoxy (Kurtz 1991, 180). It was "the dawn of a renewed awareness of human limitation" (Kurtz 1987, 451). A.A. and the Twelve Step philosophy accepted human imperfection, repudiated absolute control by the individual, advocated dependence on resources beyond the self, and offered a distinctive remedy to existential shame that "constitute a benchmark in the modern history of ideas" (White 2014, 212). Contrary to popular belief, A.A. has never represented itself as a self-help program. As White clarifies, "the source of strength that propels the A.A. member's movement into recovery is not within the self, but in resources outside the self. As such, A.A. is the antithesis of self-help" (White 2014, 191). He concludes that A.A. is "the yardstick by which all other such societies are measured" (White 2003, 26).

Aldous Huxley, author of *Brave New World* (Huxley 1932), credits Bill Wilson with being "the greatest social architect of the century" (Alcoholics Anonymous World Services 1984, 368), and *Life* magazine named him "among the one hundred most important figures of the twentieth century" (Hartigan 2000, 4). M. Scott Peck, the author of *The Road Less Travelled* (Peck 2003), offers this testimonial: "I believe, along with many other people, that perhaps the greatest event of the 20th Century occurred in 1935 in Akron, Ohio, when A.A. was established" (Peck 2013, accessed September 2014). White concludes his discussion of the history of treatment with this assessment of A.A.:

> No recovery mutual-aid movement before or after A.A. has reached more alcoholics, achieved greater geographical dispersion, been more widely adapted to address other problems, sustained itself so long, nor more profoundly influenced the evolution of addiction treatment.... [It] did not require scarce federal, state, or municipal funds—or equally scarce personal financial resources. It had to be a movement that could achieve credibility with alcoholics. It had to be a movement that altered America's very conception of the alcoholic. It had to be a movement that could last. The movement that came met all of these criteria. (White 2014, 169)

A.A. has been referred to as "the only continuing and successful group dealing with alcoholism" (Madsen 1974, 156), and "the most significant event in the whole history of alcoholism treatment" (Conley and Sorensen 1971, 113). Howard J. Clinebell Jr. remarks, "In all the long, dark, dismal history of the problem of alcoholism, the brightest ray of hope and help is Alcoholics Anonymous" (Clinebell 1998, 195). As Dubiel recognizes, "Rooted in humility and informed by a Higher Power, the strength of A.A. fellowship has endured when this fad or that had passed" (Dubiel 2004, 142–43). The third edition of the *Big Book* states that, "Of alcoholics who came to A.A. and really tried, 50% got sober at once and remained that way; 25% sobered up after some relapses, and among the remainder, those who stayed on with A.A. showed improvement" (Alcoholics Anonymous World Services 1976, xx). It is estimated that as many as 10 percent of adults in the United States will attend meetings of Alcoholics Anonymous (Miller 2010, 111). According to a membership survey by A.A., there are approximately one hundred eighteen thousand groups in the world and two million, one hundred thousand members. Over half of these are in the United States (Alcoholics Anonymous World Services 2014, accessed September 2016). Moreover, migration from one Twelve Step program to another is not unusual. Just when we think that Alcoholics Anonymous may be approaching a saturation level in our culture, sociologist Robin Room reflects, A.A. confounds "such predictions. . . . When the history of the 20th century [sic] is written, AA [sic] will merit discussion" (Room 1993, 186).

The Role of Churches and Clergy

One of the reasons for the demise of the Washingtonians was a failure to incorporate organized religion in their approach. The Emmanuel Movement, on the other hand, was an integral part of the church in Boston by that name. The Temperance Movement had significant support from Christian churches, and the Oxford Group had roots directly in Lutheran pietism. Churches had a substantial investment in the Prohibition Movement of the early twentieth century, and the passage of Prohibition in 1920 was considered a crowning achievement for American Protestantism (Conley and Sorensen 1971, 5).

With the failure and repeal of Prohibition in 1933, Sydney E. Ahlstrom recounts, churches "beheld the great victory being undone. . . . It was the greatest blow to their pride and self-confidence that Protestants . . . had ever experienced" (Ahlstrom 1972, 925). Another writer observes that the repeal of Prohibition caused churches to "drift away from this issue, as much from dejection as rejection" (Mercadante 1966a, 9). Less than three years later, in the midst of the Great Depression, Alcoholics Anonymous

ANONYMOUS CHRISTIANS

was born,[2] and "picked up the torch dropped by the church" (Mercadante 1996a, 4). Churches never again resumed leadership in the crusade against addiction. In the mid-twentieth century, Kurtz notes, there was a "transfer of social authority from revealed religions to moralizing psychologies" (Kurtz 1991, 180). Another observer puts it succinctly: "In the realm of addictions AA [sic] controls the discussion, even within the church" (Welch 2001, 5). In general, churches have neglected to develop a theology to deal with addiction and help addicts from a biblical perspective.[3] Mercadante emphasizes, "It is time to treat this allergy. That can only happen if religion rejoins the discussion" (Mercadante 1998, 314).

Nonetheless, there was a handful of clergy who continued in the discussion and were faithful in their support of Alcoholics Anonymous. The leader of the Oxford Group in America was Samuel M. Shoemaker, the Anglican rector of the Calvary Episcopal Church in New York City. Shoemaker operated a rescue mission for the drunk and homeless, sponsored meetings of the Oxford Group in the Calvary House, and was a staunch supporter of A.A. Wilson said of him, "It is through Sam Shoemaker that most of A.A.'s spiritual principles have come. . . . [He is] one of the great channels, one of the prime sources of influence, that have gathered themselves together into what is now A.A." (Alcoholics Anonymous World Services 1957, 261). Many of the principles from Shoemaker's volume, *The Conversion of the Church: The Genius of Fellowship* (Shoemaker 2008), apply to A.A. As Shoemaker says, "the primary work of the Church is the re-making of the inner lives of individuals" (Shoemaker 2008, 13). Decrying the doctrine of the Social Gospel, Shoemaker preached a pietistic message: "God's will is sometimes made clear, also, by circumstances. He guides by open and closed doors" (Shoemaker 2008, 55). As is true of A.A., the church at its best is a fellowship: "There was in the Early Church something called the '*koinonia*,' the fellowship. Its precise relation to the *ecclesia*—the Church— is not known. . . . Christians have always known and met this need when Christianity was alive and shining" (Shoemaker 2008, 83; italics his). For Shoemaker, community is the one thing that can offset the sin of pride. The church fails when it is simply an institution. As with A.A., it needs to be a

---

2. Bill Wilson got sober in December 1934. The date of Dr. Bob's last drink, and thus the birth of A.A., is traditionally considered to be June 10, 1935, but recent historical research suggests it was probably June 17, 1935 (White 2014, 173).

3. It should be noted, however, that in the late twentieth century, John Baker and Rick Warren of the Saddleback Church designed a Christ-centered Twelve Step derivative, Celebrate Recovery.

INTRODUCTION

quiet place "of unhurried people with time enough for souls" (Shoemaker 2008, 107).

Harry Emerson Fosdick, minister of the inter-denominational Riverside Church in Manhattan, spoke in support of Alcoholics Anonymous at a banquet sponsored by John D. Rockefeller in 1940, and wrote a favorable review of the *Big Book* in which he stated: "The book is not in the least sensational. It is notable for its sanity, restraint, and freedom from overemphasis and fanaticism. It is a sober, careful, tolerant, sympathetic treatment of the alcoholic's problem and of the successful techniques by which its co-authors have won their freedom" (Alcoholics Anonymous World Services 1957, 322–23). Wilson acknowledged that Fosdick "beautifully reviewed the book, just as he promised" (Alcoholics Anonymous World Services 1957, 173). Fosdick then endorsed A.A. in his book, *The Living of These Days: An Autobiography* (Fosdick 1956): "Alcoholics Anonymous has grown to its present astonishing strength, and it is a godsend to us ministers" (Fosdick 1956, 287).

Walter F. Tunks was the rector at St. Paul's Protestant Episcopal Church in Akron, Ohio. He was the clergyman that Wilson serendipitously telephoned from the Mayflower Hotel when Bill needed to find another alcoholic with whom to talk. Tunks gave him the name of Henrietta Seiberling, who in turn led Wilson to his historic meeting with Dr. Bob Smith. In the following years, Dr. Bob became a communicant at St. Paul's, and Tunks officiated at his funeral in 1950. On November 26, 1939, Unitarian minister Dilworth Lupton gave a sermon in Cleveland, titled, "Mr. X and Alcoholics Anonymous," describing the leader of A.A. in that community, Clarence Snyder. The positive publicity in the press, as well as support from the pulpit, contributed to unprecedented growth of A.A. in Cleveland.

Roman Catholic figures contributed as well. The best known was Fr. Edward Dowling, SJ, who became Bill's non-alcoholic sponsor. Dowling wrote the first Catholic recommendation of A.A., and his continuing efforts on behalf of A.A. were prodigious. Wilson offered this tribute to Father Ed:

> In my entire acquaintance, our friend Father Ed is the only one from whom I have never heard a resentful word and of whom I have never heard a single criticism. In my own life he has been a friend, adviser, great example, and the source of more inspiration than I can say. Father Ed is made of the stuff of the saints. (Alcoholics Anonymous World Services 1957, 254)

Other priests such as Ralph S. Pfau (also known as Fr. John Doe), John Dillon, Raymond Atkins, and John C. Ford, SJ, were notable in their early support of A.A. and the founding of the National Clergy Conference on Alcoholism in 1949. Serving in the alcoholic ward of hospitals, Sister Ignatia, Sister Victorine, and Sister Francis were a source of inspiration and hope. Sister Ignatia worked closely with Dr. Bob in admitting alcoholics to St. Thomas Hospital in Akron. Her practice of giving every discharged patient a Sacred Heart badge was a forerunner of A.A.'s practice of presenting medallions for periods of sobriety.

Those few clergy who supported A.A., however, were the exception rather than the rule. The problem today is that many clergy, as well as most churches, have distanced themselves from addiction recovery and by default left the matter to the Twelve Step movement. This writer has conducted field research, including surveys and interviews of clergy in the Florida Keys, to determine the current knowledge level and attitude of clergy regarding Twelve Step programs. Next, he included this information toward the development of a graduate-level course syllabus providing training for pastors and those in ministerial training on addiction and the Twelve Step process.

RELATIONSHIP OF THE TOPIC TO THE MINISTRY OF THE WRITER

This writer, a retired pastor, has carried on an addiction recovery ministry for forty-five years. In this capacity, he has mentored, taught, and prayed with hundreds of men suffering from addiction. When he moved to the Florida Keys in 1994, he attended numerous churches in an effort to find a church home, but criticism and lack of support from pastors for Twelve Step programs disappointed him. He resolved to learn more about the relationship of churches to addiction recovery, and eventually chose that as the subject for this study. In particular, he welcomed the opportunity to explore the topic through systematic field research.

Therefore, he has a passion for both the church and addiction recovery. He is a member of the Ministerial Association of the Upper Keys and has been active in the field of addictionology in South Florida. He was recently a speaker at the "Resilience in Addiction Recovery Symposium" at Baptist Hospital of Miami, chaired by Dr. John C. Eustace of the South Miami Hospital Addiction Treatment and Recovery Center. Finally, he has

INTRODUCTION

been a college professor for nearly 50 years and has both experience in teaching and familiarity with syllabus design, which he utilized in the application stage of this study.

SCOPE AND LIMITATIONS

The scope of this research was to determine the views of clergy toward the Twelve Step model in ministry and the development of a syllabus for remedial training in addiction recovery. As noted, such a study reflected this writer's personal ministry concern for those suffering from addiction. The research was limited to clergy in the Florida Keys, and was further limited to pastors who are active in the Upper Keys Ministerial Association and the Key West Alliance of Ministers.[4] Thus, the current study involved a non-probability sample. The inquiry did not consider the problem of addiction in general—only as Twelve Step programs address it. This researcher administered a survey to twenty-seven clergy; in addition, there were follow-up interviews with fourteen pastors.

Assumptions of this study included the following:

1. Pastors and those in training are often not well informed about current thinking in addictionology.
2. They may have unfavorable attitudes toward Twelve Step methodology.
3. They are sometimes not well equipped to cope with addiction issues among parishioners.
4. The surveys and interviews would be so designed as to provide results that would inform the writing of a syllabus on Twelve Step strategy for pastors or those in ministerial training.
5. Those participating in this study would range in their theological orientation from Unitarian to fundamentalist.
6. The proposed syllabus and course would be helpful to clergy. This study was limited to the planning phase of the syllabus and did not include its implementation.

---

4. A recent survey by the University of Washington shows residents of the Florida Keys drink "at higher rates than . . . Miami neighbors, or any other Florida county. . . . These estimates should be used as an aid in designing and implementing targeted interventions" (Gore 2015, accessed February 2016).

15

Relevant definitions included the following:

1. Addiction is "any compulsive, habitual behavior that limits the freedom of human desire" (May 1991, 24). More specifically, addiction is a drive to take a substance or engage in a behavior "combined with an impaired ability to control that urge, even in the face of well known adverse, even catastrophic consequences" (Volkow and Warren 2014, 3).
2. Addictionology is the study and treatment of addiction.
3. Twelve Step philosophy follows the process originated by A.A. found in the book *Alcoholics Anonymous* (Alcoholics Anonymous World Services 1955, 59–60).
4. Twelve Step groups are addiction recovery programs that follow the Twelve Step philosophy above, now numbering over fifty derivatives from A.A., including Al-Anon, Narcotics Anonymous (N.A.), and Overeaters Anonymous (O.A.).[5]
5. Christ-centered Twelve Step groups follow the Twelve Step philosophy above and specifically identify Jesus Christ as their Higher Power. They include programs such as Celebrate Recovery, Overcomers Outreach, and Alcoholics Victorious.

GOALS AND OBJECTIVES

This study had four primary goals. The objectives of these goals, which are both cognitive and affective, are listed in bullet form. The first goal was to understand the preconditions that influence the view of pastors toward the Twelve Step paradigm.

- To ascertain the role of family history and personal experience with addiction among clergy in their reaction to Twelve Step groups
- To consider the influence, if any, of age and gender of clergy in their perception of Twelve Step programs
- To determine the impact of denominational affiliation on views of clergy toward Twelve Step organizations

---

5. There is even a secular version of the Twelve Step movement known as We Agnostics, Atheists and Free-Thinkers International Alcoholics Anonymous (WAAFT).

- To reflect on whether the level of seminary training and other education, notably in social sciences, has an effect upon knowledge of the Twelve Step position

The second goal of this work was to ascertain how informed pastors are about addiction and the Twelve Step format.

- To establish how knowledgeable pastors are on the problem of addiction
- To determine how familiar pastors are with the Twelve Step philosophy
- To explore how aware clergy are of Christ-based Twelve Step groups
- To ascertain the perception of pastors about church members who have active addictions

The third goal of this research was to determine the attitudes of clergy, specifically how favorable they are toward the Twelve Step model.

- To study whether clergy perceive addiction as a sin or a disease, and to consider the effect of such an assessment upon their response
- To explore the extent that the Twelve Step formula is seen as based upon Christianity
- To observe ways clergy think the Twelve Step mindset departs from Christian beliefs
- To determine whether and to what extent pastors have a preference for Christ-centered Twelve Step programs

The fourth goal of this study, to which the other goals contribute, was the outcome of a course syllabus for clergy and those in ministerial training on addiction and the Twelve Step method.

- To evaluate whether the research of this study adequately informed the proposed syllabus
- The syllabus included, but was not limited to, the following: knowledge deficits in the area of addictionology as indicated by the study; history and background of Twelve Step programs; explanation of how Twelve Step organizations work; and spiritual features of the Twelve Step design and its relationship to Christianity.

Furthermore, this effort had the potential side-benefits of increasing the effectiveness of ministry to those experiencing addiction, including counseling and referral; and of clergy recognizing their own addiction issues and seeking treatment. Another application was that pastors may support increased availability of meeting space in their churches for Twelve Step groups.

Chapter 2

Theological and Biblical Perspectives

KURTZ FINDS THAT ALCOHOLICS Anonymous is a "uniquely American expression of Evangelical Pietism" (Kurtz 1991, 182). He further explains, "This first style thus stresses 'salvation' as from outside the self, and because of its root perception of awe and sense of humility is well-termed 'Pietist.' When it joyfully announces its sense and proclaims its perception as 'good news,' the style of this emphasis is also called 'Evangelical'" (Kurtz 1991, 179). Alcoholics Anonymous and the Twelve Step philosophy have never represented themselves to be a religion or a church, but rather as spiritual programs with distinct Christian origins. As such, A.A. makes no claim to possessing a unified and comprehensive theology. One observer even describes it as being "theologically unsophisticated" (Dann 2002, 67); another characterizes it as offering a "kind of 'entry-level'" or "generic form of spirituality" (Mercadante 1998, 310, 311). A.A.'s co-founder Bill Wilson acknowledges, "We are only operating a spiritual kindergarten" (Alcoholics Anonymous World Services 1967, 95). Closer examination reveals, however, that while apparently rejecting theological constructs, A.A. has in effect "retranslated them" (Mercadante 1998, 308).[1] Thus, the program of Alcoholic Anonymous is in many respects consistent with Christian spiritual traditions. Michael Hardin claims that the Twelve Steps

---

1. Mercadante enlarges on this statement: "Instead of sanctification there is the on-going recovery process. Taking the place of the church is the 'recovering community'. . . . The saints are those who make the perilous journey from addiction to recovery" (Mercadante 1998, 310–11). To this, Kurtz adds the Christian theme of pilgrimage— "A.A. storytellers are still 'on the way,' for they are ever mindful that A.A.'s promise is 'spiritual progress rather than spiritual perfection'" (Kurtz 1987, 454); and *Alcoholics Anonymous* concurs, "you will surely meet some of us as you trudge the Road of Happy Destiny" (Alcoholics Anonymous World Services 2001, 164).

> embody a paradigm basic to Christian spirituality, found in aspects of ancient and medieval Christian spiritual traditions. I would also contend that the structure of the Twelve Steps is illuminated by certain emphases of the Protestant Reformation. In this sense, the Twelve Steps are a potential ecumenical paradigm of spirituality, embracing as they do both Catholic and Protestant spiritual concerns. (Hardin 1994a, 47–48)

For example, the essence of the Twelve Steps is change, or conversion. James W. Fowler eloquently expands upon conversion as experienced in A.A.: "This conversion turns one in the direction of a core story that offers the model of a life of noncontrolling serenity, of reconciling and nondistorting relations with others and with God, and of generative investment of the self in carrying the AA [sic] message to others" (Fowler 1993, 116). A.A. tells newcomers that they only have to change "one thing"—and that is "everything." The theme of change is fundamental to A.A., is the focus of much of the Twelve Steps, and is the essence of A.A.'s spiritual experience. Carl Jung explains the spiritual experience: "Ideas, emotions, and attitudes which were once the guiding forces of the lives of these men are suddenly cast to one side, and a completely new set of conceptions and motives begins to dominate them" (Alcoholics Anonymous World Services 2001, 27).

When considering the powerlessness of addiction and the promise of recovery, certain theological issues arise, including the nature of humanity, the character of God, the role of Christ, the validity of prayer, the reality of miracles, and the place of fellowship (*koinonia*). Discussion of these issues will consider the theological and biblical principles involved, followed by their application to Twelve Step practice.

HUMANITY: SIN AND DISEASE

Addiction is about human imperfection, and theologically humanity's imperfection has been about sin. Adam and Eve could eat freely except from "the tree of the knowledge of good and evil" (Gen 2:17), but the temptation was too great for them. The story of the Fall is more than an example of disobedience; it is a commentary on the nature of addiction. Adam and Eve were not satisfied with what they had; rather, as Gerald G. May believes, "they experienced the need for more" (May 1991, 12). They were in the grips of an irresistible and insatiable craving.

Theological and Biblical Perspectives

The Meaning of Sin

Pelagius, a British monk who lived in the fourth century, stressed free will and human responsibility in personal choice. Augustine, a bishop from North Africa, recognized the role of human choice and accountability, but emphasized the binding power of sin and the need for grace. The debate between these two positions has continued through the centuries, with Christianity generally accepting the Augustinian view and the doctrine of sin.

Today sin in much of Western culture has come to reference general attitudes and postures, as much as specific behaviors. Paul Tillich considers sin to be separation or estrangement, "the personal act of turning away from that to which one belongs" (Tillich 1967, 2:46). Anna L. Peterson represents Tillich's concept of sin as "the separation of things that should be united" (Peterson 2009, 143). Another commentator points out, "Sin is not primarily about behavior, morality, nor acts. Instead, it is about one's primary orientation, telos, direction" (Mercadante 1997, 39). Sin denotes our orientation away from self, others, and God. Therefore, one form of sin is that which violates the self, and perhaps more than anything addiction is a violation of self. Hardin testifies: "In older paradigms of sin, sin was primarily a legal transgression against God and neighbor; in contemporary discussion sin is *also* seen as an attack of the self on the self. Recent studies in psychology coupled with recent biblical studies warrant such a paradigm shift" (Hardin 1994a, 51; italics his).

Application to Twelve Step Practice and Churches

A.A. literature has never been shy talking about sin. In the first chapter of *Alcoholics Anonymous,* Bill Wilson writes, "I ruthlessly faced my sins and became willing to have my new-found Friend take them away, root and branch" (Alcoholics Anonymous World Services 2001, 13). The second foundational document of A.A., *Twelve Steps and Twelve Traditions,* refers to sin a half dozen times, and specifically to the "Seven Deadly Sins" in discussing the Fourth Step on personal inventory (Alcoholics Anonymous World Services 2011, 48–49).

Six of the Twelve Steps pertain to "character defects" or "shortcomings," including self-will and selfishness, and as Wayne Grudem states, "the essence of sin is selfishness" (Grudem 1994, 491). Ego and self-centeredness are involved when considering the Third Step on surrender:

> Selfishness—self-centeredness! That, we think, is the root of our troubles. . . . So our troubles, we think, are basically of our own making. They arise out of ourselves, and the alcoholic is an extreme example of self-will run riot, though he usually doesn't think so. Above everything, we alcoholics must be rid of this selfishness. We must, or it kills us! God makes that possible. And there often seems no way of entirely getting rid of self without His aid. . . . We had to have God's help. (Alcoholics Anonymous World Services 2001, 62)

Resentment, anger, and fear are the primary focus of the Fourth Step inventory: "Resentment is the 'number one' offender. It destroys more alcoholics than anything else. From it stem all forms of spiritual disease, for we have been not only mentally and physically ill, we have been spiritually sick. When the spiritual malady is overcome, we straighten out mentally and physically" (Alcoholics Anonymous World Services 2001, 64). The two canonical A.A. texts refer to resentment and self-pity ninety-five times, and pride and anger seventy times. For the alcoholic, sin does not lie as much in excessive drinking as in accompanying moral failures. A.A. has made a unique contribution to understanding "sin talk" in our time, as William McDonough concludes: "So it would seem both that therapeutic talk about human failure is not theological and that theological talk about sin is not therapeutic. . . . AA [sic] has bridged the divide about sin-talk, giving us an approach to human failure and its healing that is both therapeutic and theological" (McDonough 2012, 40, accessed February 2016).

The medical community has increasingly supported the disease model of addiction, and it is integral to A.A. Although the word "disease" does not appear in the book, *Alcoholics Anonymous*, the term "allergy" appears three times, "malady" occurs six times, and "illness" appears ten times referring to alcoholism, including this signature passage:

> An illness of this sort—and we have come to believe it is an illness—involves those about us in a way no other human sickness can. If a person has cancer all are sorry for him and no one is angry or hurt. But not so with the alcoholic illness, for with it there goes annihilation of all the things worth while [sic] in life. (Alcoholics Anonymous World Services 2001, 18)

Historically, why have churches struggled with the subject of addiction, and often neglected this important concern? It may well be because churches have been ambivalent about whether addiction is a disease or a sin. Mercadante emphasizes the similarities between sin and addiction. She reflects that "behavior that was once called sin is often today called addiction" (Mercadante 1996a, 5), and "the addiction concept has in many ways taken over from the sin doctrine" (Mercadante 1997, 40). What we are experiencing is in effect a reframing of the sin concept. She perceives that there are

> some very distinct similarities between the *sin* and *addiction* concepts. Much borrowing has gone on. . . . In both dynamics and content, there is a relationship between the terms. This helps explain the ease with which many in the church come to embrace the addiction-recovery model. . . . The addiction-recovery metaphor has a complicated relationship to the doctrine of sin. It springs out of, replicates, replaces, and challenges it, all at the same time. (Mercadante 1996a, 6, 26; italics hers)

Other writers have observed that addiction is not merely a disease, or not simply a sin. In his book, *Not the Way It's Supposed to Be: A Breviary of Sin*, Cornelius Plantinga Jr. queries, "What really is the relationship between sin and addiction" (Plantinga 1995, 136)? He responds by saying, "addictions often include sin," and thus there is an "overlap between sin and addiction" (Plantinga 1995, 144, 146). He reflects upon whether "sinful behavior sometimes triggers the addictive process, or emerges from it, or both" (Plantinga 1995, 139).[2] Plantinga continues, "we must say neither that all addiction is simple sin nor that it is inculpable disease," but that "addictions often include sin" (Plantinga 1995, 140, 144). Finally, he concludes, "The addict therefore needs not just the God who forgives but also the God who heals" (Plantinga 1995, 149).

What then is the relationship between sin, disease, and addiction? As early as 1956, Howard J. Clinebell Jr. of the Yale School of Alcohol Studies conducted a survey of one hundred forty-six Protestant ministers at the Yale Summer School of Alcohol Studies, and found that the most frequent conceptions of the relationship between sin and alcoholism were as follows:

1. Alcoholism is a sin and not a sickness from start to finish.
2. Alcoholism begins as a personal sin and ends as a sickness.

---

2. Just as addiction can be seen as sin, Millard J. Erickson observes that sin can be considered as addictive: "Sin becomes a habit or even an addiction" (Erickson 2013, 561).

3. Alcoholism is a sickness which involves the sin of abuse.
4. Alcoholism is a sickness which is caused by a combination of factors involving both sin and sickness.
5. Alcoholism involves sin in the sense that it has destructive consequences.
6. Alcoholism is a social sin.
7. Alcoholism involves original sin. (Clinebell 1968, 168–70)

This list is replicated in Stephen P. Apthorp's book, *Alcohol and Substance Abuse* (Apthorp 1985, 55–56), and it is shortened slightly by James B. Nelson in his study *Thirst: God and the Alcoholic Experience* (Nelson 2004, 42).

E. M. Jellinek observes about Clinebell's list that "the most common view held by these clergymen is that alcoholism begins as a personal sin and ends as a sickness" (Jellinek 1960, 49). After past experience and current research, this writer tends to agree and has reached the conclusion that alcoholism/addiction may begin as a sin, but then becomes a disease. In its beginning stages, use and even abuse of alcohol or other substances/behaviors is willful and a matter of choice. At this point, it is a deliberate turning away from that to which one belongs—self, others, and God. When the use of alcohol and other things becomes habitual and out-of-control, complete with neurochemical characteristics, it becomes addiction. This view is shared by Edward T. Welch who refers to addiction as a metamorphosis from sin. He proposes, "a hybrid is emerging: addictions begin as sinful choices and end up as diseases. . . . The sin-morphing-into-disease approach seems to make sense" (Welch 2001, 37). Michael Hardin shares this position in affirming that, "Alcoholism begins as a spiritual disease, progresses to an emotional one, and ends up as a physical addiction" (Hardin 1994a, 53). This discussion of the relationship between sin, disease, and addiction will be an important aspect of the syllabus for those in ministerial training.

GOD: OMNIPOTENCE, ABUNDANCE, AND FORGIVENESS

Tillich suggests that God is the name for "that which concerns man ultimately" (Tillich 1967, 1:211). Dubiel identifies parallels between Paul Tillich and the writers of *Alcoholics Anonymous*: both "wrote much during the same period of time. . . . They both were addressing the same problem of understanding the complex being of the human person and how this person can

Theological and Biblical Perspectives

save himself or herself by surrendering to a Higher Power" (Dubiel 1999, 12, accessed December 2015). For many in recovery from addiction, what is of ultimate concern are God's power, generosity, and forgiveness.

Omnipotence

Grudem notes that God's providence is such that he "*directs, and works through,* the distinctive properties of each created thing. . . . God causes all things that happen, but . . . he does so in such a way that he somehow upholds our ability to make *willing, responsible choices*" (Grudem 1994, 319–21; italics his). The word "omnipotence" comes from the two Latin terms, *omni*, "all," and *potens*, "powerful," meaning "all-powerful." God's omnipotence means he is able to do his holy will. Scripture is a chronicle of God's power. God brings his people out of Egypt with "great power" (Ex 32:11) and "great strength" (Deut 4:37). Job declares that God's "wisdom is profound, his power is vast" (Job 9:4). Gabriel reassures Mary, "For with God nothing will be impossible" (Luke 1:37, RSV). Jesus says, "with God all things are possible" (Matt 19:26), and Paul counsels, "Finally, be strong in the Lord and in his mighty power" (Eph 6:10).

Abundance and Generosity

The story of the Gospel and the message of Christianity is one of God's extravagant generosity and bountiful provision for our needs. In Scripture, the theme of plenty and hospitality frequently plays out, a refrain that is vital in addiction recovery. In Genesis, the story of Creation is one of God as the perfect host providing the world as a place for us to be comfortable and to prosper. To this end, he created all that we need: light, water, land, vegetation, birds, fish, animals, and even a wife for Adam. In the Old Testament, God's promise is consistently one of plenty and increase. Following the story of Creation is what is referred to as the Great Mandate: "Be fruitful and increase in number; fill the earth and subdue it" (Gen 1:28), and after the Flood we are told that God will make Israel and humankind "as numerous as the stars in the sky" (Deut 10:22).

In the New Testament, the theme of abundance and hospitality continues with the Great Invitation: "Come to me, all you who are weary and burdened, and I will give you rest" (Matt 11:28). Jesus sent his disciples forth in anticipation of generosity when he told them, "Take nothing for the journey—no staff, no bag, no bread, no money, no extra tunic. Whatever house you enter, stay there until you leave that town. If people do not welcome you, shake the dust off your feet when you leave their town" (Luke 9:3–5). In the feeding of the five thousand, Christ exemplified the principle of sufficiency when he determined not to send people away hungry, and instead multiplied the loaves and fish (Luke 9:10–17). On the road to Emmaus, when the disciples met the stranger, they extended hospitality when they remarked, "Stay with us, for it is nearly evening; the day is almost over" (Luke 24:29). Christ's actions at the Last Supper embodied the spirit of hospitality and sufficiency when he washed his disciples' feet (John 13:1–17), and gave them bread and wine (Matt 26:17–30). The sacrament of Communion continues to be a reminder of God's provision and blessing. Christ depicted sufficiency and hospitality in sharing meals with tax collectors, prostitutes, and other sinners. Peter and the disciples made a point of breaking bread together, as did Paul and his followers. The commandment of Double Love portrays the principle of love that has no limits (Mark 12:30–31). The subsequent story of the Good Samaritan presents an unforgettable example of extravagant generosity and provision (Luke 10:30–35). The theology of God's sufficiency and plenty is not a frill, an embellishment, or an "add-on." It is the essence of the Christian faith, a faith based upon a God of radical generosity, who gave us no less than his beloved son that we may have life and have it abundantly.

Forgiveness and a Second Chance

God's grace and forgiveness in giving us a second chance are attributes found in both the Old and New Testaments. Moses murdered a man, but God chose him to lead his people. David committed adultery with Bathsheba and had her husband killed, but became "a man after . . . [God's] own heart" (1 Sam 13:14). Peter denied Christ and ran away, but turned out to be the leader of the church. Paul persecuted early Christians but became an apostle and author of much of the New Testament. Jesus knew that the Samaritan woman at the well had several husbands, but he befriended her. Christ said to the woman caught in adultery, "Then neither do I condemn you" (John 8:11). The allegory of the Prodigal Son illustrates that we have never fallen too low to be welcomed back to God's grace. The Prodigal Son is the story of a man lost in the world—perhaps even caught up in addiction—who "came to his senses" (Luke 15:17) and returned home. As such, it is a portrayal of *nostos*, or homecoming, a theme immortalized in Homer's *Odyssey* written in the eighth century B.C.

Application to Twelve Step Practice

In *Alcoholics Anonymous*, God is mentioned two hundred seventy-seven times by name with a capital "G," one hundred seven times with the pronouns "He," "Him," "His" and "Himself," and with such biblical names as "Creator," "Maker," and "Father," for a total of more than four hundred instances. Related concepts involve God-sufficiency, trusting God, drawing near to God, seeking first the kingdom of God, the guidance of God, humbling oneself, restitution, self-examination, admission of shortcomings, setting things right with one's brother, and witnessing. *Alcoholics Anonymous* directly quotes the Bible a number of times: "Thy will be done," "Love thy neighbor as thyself," "Faith without works is dead," and "Father of Light" (Alcoholics Anonymous World Services 2001, 88, 153, 88, 14).

In Twelve Step practice, a prime characteristic of God is his omnipotence and power. A.A.'s conception of God, sometimes identified by the New Age term "Higher Power," "came from radically individuated Protestant traditions" (Room 1993, 180). The *Big Book* insists, "But there is One who has all power—that One is God. May you find Him now" (Alcoholics Anonymous World Services 2001, 59). Several of the Twelve Steps emphasize God's role and power. Concerning the Third Step on surrender, *Alcoholics Anonymous* says: "Next, we decided that hereafter in this drama of life, God was going to be our Director. He is the Principal; we are His agents. He is the Father, and we are His children. Most good ideas are simple, and this concept was the keystone of the new and triumphant arch through which we passed to freedom" (Alcoholics Anonymous World Services 2001, 62). In discussing the Twelfth Step on spiritual awakening, *Alcoholics Anonymous* stresses, "Remind the prospect that his recovery is not dependent upon people. It is dependent upon his relationship with God" (Alcoholics Anonymous World Services 2001, 99–100).

Twelve Step literature consistently affirms dependence on God: "Actually we were fooling ourselves, for deep down in every man, woman, and child, is the fundamental idea of God" (Alcoholics Anonymous World Services 2001, 55). Moreover, "He has commenced to accomplish those things for us which we could never do by ourselves" (Alcoholics Anonymous World Services 2001, 25). In emphasizing cooperation with churches, *Alcoholics Anonymous* proclaims that "When many hundreds of people are able to say that the consciousness of the Presence of God is today the most important fact of their lives, they present a powerful reason why one should have faith" (Alcoholics Anonymous World Services 2001, 51). Members read the following passage from the chapter, "How it Works," at almost every A.A. meeting: "But there is One who has all power—that One is God. May you find Him now. . . . We asked His protection and care with complete abandon" (Alcoholics Anonymous World Services 2001, 59). The passage ends, "God could and would if He were sought" (Alcoholics Anonymous World Services 2001, 60). Such faith is nothing to be embarrassed or ashamed about: "We never apologize to anyone for depending upon our Creator. We can laugh at those who think spirituality the way of weakness. Paradoxically, it is the way of strength. . . . All men of faith have courage. They trust their God. We never apologize for God" (Alcoholics Anonymous World Services 2001, 68).

In addition to his sovereignty and power, the other attributes of God discussed above also apply to Twelve Step practice. Those who are recovering from addiction experience recovery as a manifestation of God's sufficiency and abundance. By nature, addiction endlessly seeks gratification and lacks permanent satisfaction; it is a disorder that perpetually wants more and by definition, more is never enough. Recovery reveals that God's plenty and promise are enough. At the end of the day, healing from addiction comes down to trusting God's provision. Finally, God's attribute of forgiveness and the opportunity for a second chance clearly pertain to addiction recovery. Of all that recovery represents, it means another chance at life. For the fallen alcoholic or addict, God is the god of a second chance who rejoices in our homecoming.

CHRIST: PROPHET OF HEALING

Prophets abound in the Old Testament, beginning with Moses. In the New Testament Jesus is referred to as "one of the prophets" (Luke 9:8), and his teachings about healing the sick and suffering—clearly shared in the mission of Twelve Step groups—are reflected in his role as a prophet. When he raised the son of the widow of Naim from the dead, the people said, "A great prophet has appeared among us" (Luke 7:16). The healed blind man proclaimed of Jesus, "He is a prophet" (John 9:17). When Jesus multiplied loaves and fish, some people exclaimed, "Surely this man is the Prophet"

(John 7:40). The Epistles do not refer to Christ as a prophet, perhaps because he surpasses the Old Testament prophets. Grudem suggests, "He is the one *about whom* the prophecies in the Old Testament were made. . . . [and] Jesus was not merely a messenger of revelation from God . . . but was himself the *source* of revelation from God" (Grudem 1994, 625–26; italics his). In brief, Christ's teachings about the sick and suffering validate his role as prophet and anticipate missiology concerning addiction.

A Scripture sometimes cited for helping the sick and afflicted is the passage on goats and sheep in Matthew 25:35–40, "whatever you did for one of the least of these brothers and sisters of mine, you did for me" (Matt 25:40). Although the emphasis in this passage may be upon fellow believers, Philip G. Ryken asserts, "the true test for God's servants is how they treat people whom nobody wants, nobody loves, and nobody touches because they just can't seem to get their act together" (Ryken 2003, 157). Christians are not supposed to shoot their wounded. We are to help those who suffer from addiction, because it allows us to be in touch with our own humanity, because God has commanded it, and because it confirms the truth of God's Word. The foundation for this is in John: "By this all men will know that you are my disciples, if you love one another" (John 13:35). Further on, Jesus asks Peter three times, "Do you love me?" and each time Peter affirms his love, Jesus directs him to "Feed my sheep" (John 21:17). We know that Jesus came "healing every disease and sickness among the people" (Matt 4:23).

The precedent for Christ's compassion for the suffering is in Isaiah. In the synagogue, Jesus chose to read from Isaiah 61: "He has anointed me to preach good news to the poor. He has sent me to proclaim freedom for the prisoners and recovery of sight for the blind, to release the oppressed" (Luke 4:18). Isaiah 58 likewise addresses caring for the disadvantaged: "If you spend yourselves in behalf of the hungry and satisfy the needs of the oppressed, then your light will rise in the darkness, and your night will become like the noonday" (Isa 58:10). John Piper comments, "there is something very close to Jesus' heart in Isaiah 58" (Piper 1997, 131).

Luke, however, may have the most to say about helping the marginalized. There are three parables of grace in Luke 15—the lost sheep, the lost coin, and the lost son. All three speak strongly of God who looks for the lost, and who hastens to welcome his errant children. Tim Chester and Steve Timmis affirm, "The marginalized are excluded from the blessings of this life, but the kingdom [sic] of God is a kingdom of grace, and so their lack of status, wealth, or power does not exclude them" (Chester and Timmis 2008, 72).

Application to Twelve Step Practice

Belief in Christ as a prophet of healing and the rise of Western Christianity contributed to a cultural climate for helping people with addiction. Throughout the history of Alcoholics Anonymous and the Twelve Step movement, however, there is no direct suggestion of Christology, in part to facilitate entrance into A.A. for those of different religious perspectives, or those without formal religion. As one critic observes, "neither the somewhat vague Christology of Buchman nor the more focused and theologically pervasive Christology of Shoemaker was retained by Alcoholics Anonymous.... An 'insertion' of Christ would radically change the AA program" (Mercadante 1996a, 95). Robert H. Albers justifies this omission: "The steps incorporate nearly all aspects of the faith tradition sans references to Christology. This omission of Christology has been a source of contention for those who claim allegiance to the Christian tradition, but the scope of the recovery process is a broader stroke on the canvas of life" (Albers 1997, 33). Reminiscent of the God of Israel who would not be named (Exod 3:14), Alcoholics Anonymous preferred to leave its God unnamed. As with its membership, A.A. sought to protect his anonymity.

A further application is that toward the end of the twentieth century churches began reconsidering their estrangement from addiction recovery; the result was a proliferation of Christ-centered Twelve Step groups. Welch explains their motivation: "Through the second half of the 1900s, the church lost its voice as the resource for addicts. Yet, with addiction problems growing, there are new opportunities for the church to be *the* ministering body, and more and more churches are getting serious about being instruments of change in the lives of addicts" (Welch 2001, 249; italics his). Bible-based Twelve Step groups include Overcomers Outreach, Alcoholics for Christ, Alive Again, and Alcoholics Victorious. Perhaps best known of the Christ-centered groups is Celebrate Recovery, co-authored by Rick Warren and John Baker of the Saddleback Church. These Christian Twelve Step groups have received criticism from both ends of the spectrum of opinion. There has been a backlash of criticism from some Christians. As an alternative to attending Celebrate Recovery meetings, Paul R. Stark advocates "participants become fully integrated into normal church life with the rest of the congregation"

(Stark 2004, 8, accessed May 2015). Jim Van Yperen advises, "Christianity is not a 'self-help' religion. . . . A church that organizes itself around meeting personal needs runs the great, unintended risk of breeding autonomy rather than mutuality" (Van Yperen 2002, 31). And Mercadante argues, "it is risky to place one's primary identity in a group bound by a shared pathology. . . . There are serious difficulties in making a human weakness a significant common bond" (Mercadante 1996a, 162). At the other end of the spectrum, some traditional A.A. members have reservations about Christ-centered Twelve Step programs based on their preference for having God remain anonymous. Hardin offers this caveat: "far from Christianizing the 12 Steps we must, with Bill Wilson, allow God's anonymity to remain" (Hardin 1994b, 20).

PRAYER: BETWEEN HUMANITY AND GOD

The life and teachings of Christ are a testimony to the efficacy of prayer. He says, "Ask and it will be given to you; seek and you will find" (Luke 11:9), and "I will do whatever you ask in my name. . . . You may ask me for anything in my name, and I will do it" (John 14:13–14). Grudem defines prayer as *"personal communication with God"* (Grudem 1994, 376; italics his), and W. Bingham Hunter declares that, "Prayer is communication from whole persons to the Wholeness which is the living God" (Hunter 1986, 13). Grudem notes that prayer functions on several levels. First, it "expresses our trust in God and is a means whereby our trust in him can increase. . . . [Second,] Prayer brings us into deeper fellowship with God. . . . [and Third, prayer] allows us as creatures to be involved in activities that are eternally important" (Grudem 1994, 376–77).

Application to Twelve Step Practice

Given A.A.'s Christian background, it is not surprising that Twelve Step programs place a premium on prayer. Prayer is useful in breaking the stronghold of addiction. In the introduction to *Alcoholics Anonymous*, William Duncan Silkworth expresses his hope that although the alcoholic may initially come to A.A. "to scoff, he may remain to pray" (Alcoholics Anonymous World Services 2001, xxxii). Alcoholics Anonymous insists on the practice of prayer. As William R. Miller reports, "Prayer and meditation are practiced by a majority of members on a daily basis" (Miller 2010, 128). In the fellowship of A.A., one sometimes hears the expressions, "Act as if," and "Even if you don't believe in God, pray anyway." These comments are consistent with Hunter's observation, "when we pray we don't know what we're doing" (Hunter 1986, 11).

Several specific prayers are prominent in Twelve Step practice. Members repeat the Lord's Prayer at most meetings, sometimes at the beginning but often at the conclusion of the meeting. This practice is not surprising, since "for sheer power and majesty, no prayer can equal the Paternoster" (Foster 1992, 184). A.A. includes the prayer of Saint Francis of Assisi in its literature as a model of a "really good prayer. . . . one that is a classic" (Alcoholics Anonymous World Services 2011, 99). A.A. recommends the Saint Francis prayer for study and private devotion, and members sometimes repeat and discuss it at meetings:

> Lord, make me a channel of thy peace—that where there is hatred, I may bring love—that where there is wrong, I may bring the spirit of forgiveness—that where there is discord, I may bring harmony—that where there is error, I may bring truth—that where there is doubt, I may bring faith—that where there is despair, I may bring hope—that where there are shadows, I may bring light—that where there is sadness, I may bring joy. Lord, grant that I may seek rather to comfort than to be comforted—to understand, than to be understood—to love, than to be loved. For it is by self-forgetting that one finds. It is by forgiving that one is forgiven. It is by dying that one awakens to Eternal Life. Amen. (Alcoholics Anonymous World Services 2011, 99)

The prayer most often identified with A.A., however, is the Serenity Prayer. Since the early 1940s members have recited the short form of the Serenity Prayer at virtually every A.A. meeting and it has appeared prominently in A.A. literature since the 1950s. Claimed unpretentiously as "A.A.'s simple prayer" (Alcoholics Anonymous World Services 2011, 125), it is generally attributed to the theologian Reinhold Niebuhr:[3]

> God grant me the Serenity to accept the things—[sic]I cannot change; Courage to change the things I can; and Wisdom to know the difference. Living one day at a time; Enjoying one moment at a time; Accepting hardship as the pathway to peace; Taking, as He did, this sinful world as it is, not as I would have it; Trusting that

---

3. "However, Niebuhr is quoted as crediting the prayer to Friedrich Oetinger, an 18th Century [sic] theologian" (Miller 2010, 237). Oetinger may have written the first sentence, but Niebuhr appears to have been the first to translate it into English and he may have been the author of the remaining lines (Sasser 2007, accessed October 2015).

He will make all things right if I surrender to His will; That I may be reasonably happy in this life, and supremely happy with Him forever in the next. Amen. (Wing 2009, 12, accessed December 2015)

A.A. incorporates prayer into practicing or "working" the Twelve Steps. The Third Step, turning one's life and will over to the care of God, includes an eloquent prayer of surrender: "God, I offer myself to Thee—to build with me and to do with me as Thou wilt. Relieve me of the bondage of self, that I may better do Thy will. Take away my difficulties, that victory over them may bear witness to those I would help of Thy Power, Thy Love, and Thy Way of life. May I do Thy will always" (Alcoholics Anonymous World Services 2001, 63). The Seventh Step, humbly asking God to remove defects, incorporates a specific prayer of repentance (*metanoia*): "My Creator, I am now willing that you should have all of me, good and bad. I pray that you now remove from me every single defect of character which stands in the way of my usefulness to you and my fellows. Grant me strength, as I go out from here, to do your bidding. Amen" (Alcoholics Anonymous World Services 2001, 76). The Eleventh Step is entirely devoted to prayer and meditation, seeking to "improve our conscious contact with God . . . praying only for knowledge of His will for us and the power to carry that out" (Alcoholics Anonymous World Services 2001, 59). Finally, *Alcoholics Anonymous* recommends prayer of forgiveness as a way of dealing with resentment. Its story, "Freedom from Bondage," presents a formula for dealing with anger and pride:

> If you have a resentment you want to be free of, if you will pray for the person or the thing that you resent, you will be free. If you will ask in prayer for everything you want for yourself to be given to them, you will be free. Ask for their health, their prosperity, their happiness, and you will be free. Even when you don't really want it for them and your prayers are only words and you don't mean it, go ahead and do it anyway. (Alcoholics Anonymous World Services 2001, 552)

MIRACLES: BETWEEN GOD AND HUMANITY

The life of Christ also embodied miracles. As Jesus says, "Go back and report to John what you have seen and heard: The blind receive sight, the lame walk, those who have leprosy are cured, the deaf hear, the dead are raised, and the good news is preached to the poor" (Luke 7:22). We know that a miracle is a *"less common kind of God's activity in which he arouses people's awe and wonder and bears witness to himself"* (Grudem 1994, 355; italics his). Grudem continues, miracles are "evidence that God is truly at work. . . . [they] bear witness to the fact that the kingdom of God has come. . . . [and] A third purpose of miracles is to help those who are in need" (Grudem 1994, 360).

Application to Twelve Step Practice

Addiction can be so strong that breaking its grip is felt to be nothing short of miraculous. William R. Miller affirms, "The belief in miracles has a prominent role in AA [sic] spirituality" (Miller 2010, 120), and May elaborates: "God does not wait to give us good things. . . . This is the spiritual experience I learned about from recovering addicts. . . . sudden empowerments. People who have experienced them call them miraculous" (May 1991, 153). The *Big Book* points out, "The age of miracles is still with us" (Alcoholics Anonymous World Services 2001, 153). When a sober alcoholic from the Oxford Group first carried the message of recovery to Bill Wilson, the co-founder later wrote, "My ideas about miracles were drastically revised right then. Never mind the musty past; here sat a miracle directly across the kitchen table" (Alcoholics Anonymous World Services 2001, 11). Members testify that examples of miracles include the following: finding A.A. in the first place, the act of surrender and accepting powerlessness over alcohol, freedom from the obsession to drink, becoming happy and serene, and being able to help and be of service to others. One of A.A.'s slogans is "Expect a Miracle," and the book *Alcoholics Anonymous* proclaims, "The central fact of our lives today is the absolute certainty that our Creator has entered into our hearts and lives in a way which is indeed miraculous" (Alcoholics Anonymous World Services 2001, 25). Harry M. Tiebout, psychiatric benefactor to Alcoholics Anonymous, emphasized that those in recovery need discipline as well as miracles. Important as the miraculous aspect of recovery is, he stipulates, "A.A. can never be just a miracle." If the alcoholic in recovery does not stay centered and disciplined, he may need another miracle "which may not come off the next time" (Alcoholics Anonymous World Services 1957, 250–1).

KOINONIA: EMPOWERMENT OF FELLOWSHIP

An aspect of ecclesiology, community, or fellowship is conveyed by the Greek word *koinonia*. Van Yperen considers the derivation of the word: "*Community, communion,* and *communicate* all come from the same Greek root word, *koinonia*, meaning to 'hold things in common,' or 'joint participation,' most commonly translated as 'fellowship'" (Van Yperen 2002, 203; italics his). After creating man, God observed, "It is not good for the man to be alone" (Gen 2:18). Significantly, "the only thing in all creation that is not good is the man on his own" (Chester and Timmis 2008, 40). Trying to live in the image of God *(imago Dei)* means being in relationship with each other: "The image of God is a relational image. We, together, constitute the image of God. As isolated individuals, we are but a fracture of that image. To be made in the image of God is to be made in relationship" (Hardin 1994a, 49).

When asked when the Kingdom of God was coming Jesus answered, "the kingdom of God is in the midst of you" (Luke 17:21, RSV). God is in relationship; in a mystical sense, he is relationship itself. Fellowship was as significant to the apostle Paul as it was to Jesus and his disciples. Paul's "band of brothers" included Prisca and Aquila, Urbanus, Timothy, Epaphroditus, Euodia, Syntyche, Clement, Epaphras, Tychicus, Archippus, and Phoebe. Clearly, God is in community and fellowship. Gerald G. May testifies to the value of the "lasting steadiness" of communities of faith: "When I cannot pray, the prayer of countless others goes on. Where I am complacent, others are struggling. Where I am in conflict, others are at peace. Most important, when I cannot act in loving ways, there are those in my communities who can" (May 1991, 175).

Application to Twelve Step Practice

In words as visionary for Twelve Step groups as for churches, James W. Thompson proposes: "Our pastoral ambition is to build the community in the context of the threats posed by the gods of our own age" (Thompson 2006, 148). Shoemaker testifies to the value of community in spiritual growth:

> From the first, Christ drew about Him a company. To join Him, you had also to join that company. The church has always been a scratch company of sinners. It is not the best people in the community gathered together for self-congratulation; it is the people

who know they have a great need gathered to find its answer in worship toward God and fellowship with one another. The church is not a museum; it is a hospital. (Alcoholics Anonymous World Services 1957, 268)

From its inception, Alcoholics Anonymous intuitively grasped the value of fellowship. The Preamble of A.A. states, "Alcoholics Anonymous is a fellowship of men and women who share their experience, strength and hope with each other that they may solve their common problem and help others to recover from alcoholism" (AA Grapevine 2013, accessed February 2016). The book, *Alcoholics Anonymous,* offers this assurance:

> Life will take on new meaning. To watch people recover, to see them help others, to watch loneliness vanish, to see a fellowship grow up about you, to have a host of friends—this is an experience you must not miss. We know you will not want to miss it. Frequent contact with newcomers and with each other is the bright spot of our lives. (Alcoholics Anonymous World Services 2001, 89)

In 1940, New York philanthropist Albert Scott observed A.A.'s practices of abstinence and fasting from alcohol, daily meetings for prayer and edification, seeking God's will, breaking bread together, mutual encouragement, and fellowship. He declared flatly, "Why, this is first-century Christianity" (Alcoholics Anonymous World Services 1984, 184).

SUMMARY

The theological and biblical issues surveyed in this chapter have included the nature of humanity, the character of God, the role of Christ, the validity of prayer, the reality of miracles, and the place of fellowship (or *koinonia*). A.A. and the Twelve Step philosophy have significant roots in Christian theology and in Scripture. Addiction is about human imperfection and prompts discussion about traditional views of sin and contemporary perspectives of moral failure and disease. The remedy lies in God's power, generosity, and forgiveness. Christ is a prophet helping those who are afflicted and suffer. Diversity exists between Christ-centered Twelve Step groups and those who opt for having God remain anonymous. Regardless of the conception of a Higher Power, prayer is the life-blood of recovery. Miracles are the stuff of which recovery is made, and fellowship (*koinonia*) is the nesting place of healing and growth.

Chapter 3

Issues from Related Contemporary Literature

A THOROUGH REVIEW OF the extant literature on this subject was conducted. It was with some satisfaction that this writer researched and compiled the bibliography or reference list of this study. Many fine minds are represented, including Ernest Kurtz, William L. White, William R. Miller, Robin Room, Linda A. Mercadante, Gerald G. May, and Howard J. Schaffer. They do not always agree, but this writer is indebted to the combined wisdom they offer. It is now this researcher's task to review the current literature, to observe patterns of development and thought, and to see how the authors interact in contributing to this work as a whole.

The final goal of this study was the outcome of a course syllabus for clergy and those in ministerial training on addiction and the Twelve Step method. One objective of this goal was the inclusion of the following elements or issues in the syllabus: (1) Knowledge deficits in the area of addictionology as indicated by the study, (2) History and background of Twelve Step programs, (3) Explanation of how Twelve Step organizations work, (4) Spiritual features of the Twelve Step design and its relationship to Christianity, (5) Current information on addiction theory, and (6) The general subject of addiction treatment. This chapter lays the groundwork for such a syllabus by reviewing contemporary literature that pertains to each of these issues.

LITERATURE ON KNOWLEDGE DEFICITS IN ADDICTIONOLOGY

Some contemporary literature addresses the issue of clergy knowledge deficits in addictionology. In 2001, the Substance Abuse and Mental Health Administration joined with the National Association for Children of Alcoholics and the Johnson Institute in convening an expert panel on seminary training on addiction. They found that offerings of schools of theology vary greatly, with "few offering specific instruction focused on working with parishioners troubled with alcohol or drug use" (National Association 2003, 1). They concluded that at the time of their study, "the environment in seminaries today is not conducive to expanding the offerings in this field" (National Association 2003, 21).

In an unprecedented two-year study, the National Center on Addiction and Substance Abuse at Columbia University surveyed clergy in the field and presidents of seminaries and schools of theology, and echoed the above findings. Their report found that 94.4 percent of clergy recognized that addiction is a major problem in their congregations, but only 12.5 percent had completed any coursework on the topic (National Center on Addiction 2001, 20–21). Almost all of the seminary presidents (97.6 percent) "rated substance abuse as very important," but just 25.8 percent reported that students were required to take addiction courses (National Center on Addiction 2001, 20, 3). A disconnect from the problem of addiction was especially noticeable in preaching. Only 36.5 percent of clergy reported that they preached a sermon on addiction more than once annually—and 22.4 percent never preached on the topic (National Center on Addiction 2001, 22). This report recommended that seminaries "include courses related to substance abuse in degree requirements and provide in-service training for current clergy" (National Center on Addiction 2001, 3). The findings of this study were restated in an article, "Religion, Spirituality, and the Troublesome Use of Substances," by Keith Humphreys and Elizabeth Gifford who report, "clergy seldom receive training in pastoral counseling for substance use" (Humphreys and Gifford, 2006, 268). They conclude:

> Religious leaders may educate clergy in substance abuse treatment and delivery, and network with mental health providers. . . . scientists must be willing to ask scientific questions about the role of religion/spirituality in addiction and recovery, and religious leaders must value the scientific process and its rigorous humility. (Humphreys and Gifford 2006, 272)

Issues from Related Contemporary Literature

This researcher finds the results of the study by the National Association for Children of Alcoholics and the Johnson Institute, and the study by the National Council on Addiction and Substance Abuse at Columbia University to be serendipitous, and in themselves validate this current research and the development of a syllabus for seminary use. C. Roy Woodruff reacts to these two studies in his article, "Role of the Clergy: The Effects of Alcohol and Drugs on the Person and the Family" (Woodruff 2003, 8–13). He reports that the specified research found that "clergy in many if not most major U.S. religious faith groups and denominations feel poorly equipped to deal with the problem as it presents itself in their congregations" (Woodruff 2003, 9). The lack of preparation can directly attributed to the following:

> Offerings of today's clergy training institutions vary greatly, with some institutions providing little specific instruction on the subject, and only a few offering complete curricula on addiction. In seminaries accredited by the Association of Theological Schools in the U.S. and Canada, most students enrolled in generalist programs receive little specialized training; at most, an elective course. (Woodruff 2003, 10)

Woodruff suggests several reasons for the outcome of these studies. "A surface explanation is competition for space in the curriculum.... Addiction is a complex, difficult subject, and it may not seem feasible to do it justice." (Woodruff 2003, 9). Another explanation is that areas such as "biochemistry, counseling and treatment" in the current model of addiction have become the province of health professionals (Woodruff 2003, 9). Ironically, there appears to be a similar bias in the minds of health professionals, who "acknowledge that religion and spirituality are important aids to recovery," but who defer them to clergy (Woodruff 2003, 9). Clearly, what is needed are interdisciplinary courses in seminaries. Of course they will be in competition with other subjects, but the significance of the issue warrants that they be seriously considered.

LITERATURE ON HISTORY AND BACKGROUND OF TWELVE STEP PROGRAMS

In the development of a syllabus, the second issue pertains to the history and background of Twelve Step programs. Writers have struggled for some time to explain addiction. Benjamin Rush's treatise represents an early effort to confront the perils of alcoholism. Yet Rush's best suggestion was the substitution of beer and wine for distilled spirits (Rush 2011, 16–18). For nearly one hundred years, it was as if his words fell on deaf ears. Then in the early twentieth century, writers began to find their voice with Richard Peabody's book, *The Common Sense of Drinking* (Peabody 1930). An outcome of the Emmanuel Movement in Boston, it dealt with alcoholism as a treatable condition. This volume was read eagerly by Bill Wilson, and it was background material when he wrote *Alcoholics Anonymous* in 1938. Richard M. Dubiel joined the discussion by documenting the Emmanuel Movement's contribution to Alcoholics Anonymous in his book, *The Road to Fellowship: The Role of the Emmanuel Movement and the Jacoby Club in the Development of Alcoholics Anonymous* (Dubiel 2004). Paul C. Conley and Andrew A. Sorensen presented an overview of the subject in *The Staggering Steeple: The Story of Alcoholism and the Churches* (Conley and Sorensen 1971), which commented on the relationship of churches and alcoholism in Colonial America, through the Temperance Movement, and into the Prohibition era.

William L. White responded with a chapter on "Alcoholic Mutual Aid Societies" that was published in the book *Alcohol and Temperance in Modern History* edited by Jack S. Blocker et al. (White 2003, 24–27). A pre-cursor to his volume on addiction treatment published in 2014, White testifies that through the 1830s Americans suffering from alcoholism "sought shelter within a rising temperance movement" (White 2003, 24). Following temperance, a number of mutual aid resources appeared, culminating in Alcoholics Anonymous in 1935. A.A. dominated the recovery scene until the mid-1970s when Christianized Twelve Step programs began to appear, as well as adaptations of the Twelve Step programs for problems other than alcohol. Katherine McCarthy was of the same mind in publishing a comprehensive article, "Early Alcoholism Treatment: The Emmanuel Movement and Richard Peabody" (McCarthy 1984, 59–74). In it, she details the antecedents of A.A., including the Washingtonian Movement of the 1840s, and she documents the roles of Courtenay Baylor and Richard Peabody in the Emmanuel Movement.

A.A.'s roots, however, were directly in the Oxford Group, and it was from here that A.A. had its origin as a Christian fellowship. The Oxford Group's character as a Christian parachurch organization is clarified in Garth Lean's biography of Oxford Group founder, Frank Buchman, titled *On the Tail of a Comet: The Life of Frank Buchman* (Lean 1988), and other biographies of Buchman such as that by Peter Howard, *Frank Buchman's Secret* (Howard 1961). Samuel M. Shoemaker, an Episcopal rector, was

Issues from Related Contemporary Literature

the acknowledged leader of the Oxford Group in America, and his publication in 1932 of *The Conversion of the Church: The Genius of Fellowship* (Shoemaker 2008) reads into the record the Christian heritage of both the Oxford Group and Alcoholics Anonymous. John F. Woolverton's article, "Evangelical Protestantism and Alcoholism 1933–1962" (Woolverton 1983, 153–65), summarizes the relationship of the Oxford Group, Shoemaker, and Alcoholics Anonymous. It is vital to be aware of the history and background of Twelve Step programs, and we are indebted to an abundance of writers such as Peabody, Dubiel, Conley and Sorensen, Shoemaker, and more recently to McCarthy, White, and Woolverton for providing historical continuity to early addiction recovery.

The Christian origins of Alcoholics Anonymous are explained from A.A.'s point of view in the volume, *Alcoholics Anonymous Comes of Age* (Alcoholics Anonymous World Services 1957), which represents a comprehensive history of Alcoholics Anonymous. This is a faithful and indispensable historical survey. It includes an account of the historic Twentieth Anniversary Convention of Alcoholics Anonymous in St. Louis in 1955, during which Bill Wilson officially placed the leadership of A.A. into the hands of its members and elected representatives. At the closing session, Wilson eloquently thanked God for helping A.A.:

> [He] had directed us to construct this cathedral whose foundations already rest upon the corners of the earth. On its great floor 200,000 of us are now sustained in peace. . . . The older ones among us have seen the side walls of this cathedral going up, and one by one they have seen the buttresses of the A.A. Tradition set in place to contain us in unity for so long as God may will it so. And now eager hearts and hands have lifted the spire of our cathedral into place. That spire bears the name of Service. May it ever point straight upward toward God. (Alcoholics Anonymous World Services 1957, 234)

Only five years earlier in 1950, at the Fifteenth Anniversary Convention, Dr. Bob Smith made his last public appearance shortly before he died. Summing all of his strength, he remarked, "Our Twelve Steps, when simmered down to the last, resolve themselves into the words 'love' and 'service'" (Alcoholics Anonymous World Services 1980, 338).

William Madsen's commentary, *The American Alcoholic: The Nature-Nurture Controversy in Alcoholic Research and Therapy* (Madsen 1974), expresses a conceptual overview of A.A. However, the most astute analysis may be found in Ernest Kurtz's *Not-God: A History of Alcoholics Anonymous* (Kurtz 1991), first published in 1979. The book is an outcome of his PhD dissertation completed at Harvard University in 1978, written from the perspective of American history and in the context of the history of religious ideas. Kurtz, who was not a member of A.A., had "full and complete access to the archives of the General Service Office of Alcoholics Anonymous in New York. . . . [and conducted] extensive interviews of surviving early members and friends of A.A." (Kurtz 1991, About the Book). From his vantage point, Kurtz discusses the limitations of the drinking alcoholic, the sober alcoholic, and Alcoholics Anonymous itself.

Adding to the dialogue is Kurtz's article, "Alcoholics Anonymous and the Disease Concept of Alcoholism," prepared for publication in the *Alcoholism Treatment Quarterly* (Kurtz 2002). This fifty-eight-page article was subsidized by a grant originating from the Illinois Department of Human Services Office of Alcoholism and Substance Abuse, and represents an exploration of A.A. literature and history on the attitude of A.A. toward addiction as a disease. Kurtz's part in the discussion included a chapter in *Religion and Philosophy in the U.S.A.* titled, "Alcoholics Anonymous: A Phenomenon in American History" (Kurtz 1987, 447–62), in which he observes that there was both climate and soil of opinion for the origin of A.A. He concludes that the rise of existentialist philosophy and neo-orthodox theology was vital, even if "less significant, for our purposes, than the Great Depression, the revelations of Auschwitz, and the use of atomic weapons" (Kurtz 1987, 451). Ernest Kurtz occupies a singular position as the acknowledged historian of record for A.A. His work is a touchstone by which other historical accounts are judged.

Background on A.A. and Twelve Step programs is also conveyed by intensive studies of Bill Wilson in biographies by Robert Thomsen, *Bill W.* (Thomsen 1975); and by Alcoholics Anonymous World Services, *"Pass it on:" The Story of Bill Wilson and How the A.A. Message Reached the World* (Alcoholics Anonymous World Services 1984). Second generation biographies of Wilson by Francis Hartigan (2000) and by Susan Cheever (2004) offer additional historical perspective. Biographies by Thomsen and A.A. World Services are comprehensive, but those by Hartigan and Cheever come later and provide more objectivity on Wilson's shortcomings such as his depression, recreational LSD use, and marital infidelity. Alcoholics Anonymous World Services provides a comprehensive and affectionate view of its less controversial co-founder Dr. Bob Smith in its biography, *Dr.*

Issues from Related Contemporary Literature

Bob and the Good Oldtimers: A Biography with Recollections of Early A.A. in the Midwest (Alcoholics Anonymous World Services 1980).

William L. White and Ernest Kurtz, who were friends as well as collaborators, spoke with one voice in their article "Twelve Defining Moments in the History of Alcoholics Anonymous," published in *Recent Developments in Alcoholism* (White and Kurtz 2008, 37–57). This article addresses the seminal moments in A.A.'s history: (1) Jung's refusal to treat Roland Hazard; (2) Wilson's "Hot Flash," Wilson's panic at the Mayflower Hotel; (3) the temptation of professionalism; (4) the question of A.A. membership requirements; (5) Rockefeller's warnings about money; (6) the split from the Oxford Group; (7) formalizing of the Twelve Steps; (8) growing pains; (9) alcoholism treatment as a business; (10) the split-off of Marty Mann's National Committee for Education on Alcoholism; (11) the writing of the Twelve Traditions; (12) and the separation of institutional treatment. This article is an excellent summary of key points in A.A. history.

There are a number of accounts by members of A.A., who in the spirit of anonymity identify themselves by first name and last initial only. Dick B. entered the dialogue with his history of early A.A. titled, *The James Club and the Original A.A. Program's Absolute Essentials* (B., Dick 2005). In conjunction with Bill Pittman, Dick B. produced a volume, *Courage to Change: The Christian Roots of the Twelve-Step Movement* (Pittman and Dick B. 1994), which chronicles A.A.'s relationship to Sam Shoemaker and the Oxford Group. With a foreword by Ann Smith and Bob Smith Jr., Dick B. presented a study, *The Good Book and the Big Book* (B., Dick 1997), which reflected the parallels between the Bible and *Alcoholics Anonymous*. These works are passionate, but stem as much from participation in Twelve Step groups as from traditional scholarship.

In summary, there is a plethora of literature on the history and background of the Twelve Step movement, stemming from histories by Kurtz and White to biographies of Bill Wilson and Dr. Bob Smith. The works are uniformly enthusiastic, if not always academically rigorous. They provide fertile ground for study of the history of addiction recovery in the projected course syllabus.

LITERATURE EXPLAINING HOW TWELVE STEP ORGANIZATIONS WORK

Given clergy's knowledge deficits on addiction and the background of Twelve Step groups, the next issue to consider is how Twelve Step programs work. Alcoholics Anonymous is considered the primary Twelve Step model not only because it was the original version, but as William White and Ernst Kurtz observe, "[It] has earned its place as the benchmark by which all other mutual aid groups are compared" (White and Kurtz 2008, 38). Other authors are so much in agreement on the unique role of A.A., it is almost as if they are speaking with one voice. William Madsen comments in his book, *The American Alcoholic*, that "A.A. is the only continuing and successful group dealing with alcoholism" (Madsen 1974, 156). Daniel Dubiel's book states that A.A. "has endured when this fad or that had passed" (Dubiel 2004, 143), and Edward T. Welch declares that "In the realm of addictions AA [sic] controls the discussion, even within the church" (Welch 2001, 5).

The *Big Book*

Discussion of the current literature review culminates in consideration of the book, *Alcoholics Anonymous*, from which the A.A. fellowship took its name.[1] Affectionately referred to by members as the *Big Book*, it is now in its fourth edition. It is the consummation of the dialogue in this country from the writings of Benjamin Rush to the experience with Temperance and Prohibition and includes themes drawn overtly from the Emmanuel Movement and the Oxford Group. The publication of this book was instrumental in the meteoric growth of A.A., as White and Kurtz reflect, "The dissemination of the book, *Alcoholics Anonymous*, played a pivotal role in spreading AA's [sic] message" (White and Kurtz 2008, 48). Bill Wilson, co-founder of A.A., was the anonymous author,[2] and Tom Uzzell of *Collier's* magazine acted as unofficial editor. First published

---

1. Another name considered for the new fellowship was the "James Club," because of the popularity of the Book of James and its frequently quoted passage, "Faith without works is dead" (Jas 2:20 KJV). The name given to A.A.'s new publishing enterprise, "Works Publishing Inc.," may have come from this source.

2. Wilson even wrote the chapters titled, "To Wives" and "The Family Afterward." His wife, Lois, expected to be asked to write these chapters, but Bill said, "he thought the book, except for the stories, should all be written in the same style" (Wilson 1979, 114). However, another member's wife, Marie Blay, might have written the first draft of the chapter, "To Wives."

in April 1939, the style of *Alcoholics Anonymous* has been termed "anachronistic and overly sentimental" (McCarthy 1984, 72), and Kurtz has characterized Wilson's manner as sometimes being "preachy" (Kurtz 1991, 71). The other co-founder, Dr. Bob Smith of Akron, played a less active role in the publication and organizational responsibilities of A.A. As Thomsen says in his biography of Wilson, "Perhaps AA [sic] needed them both, the quiet doctor who kept his inner life simple, and Bill W., to whom nothing was ever simple" (Thomsen 1975, 347).

For this writer, the very heart of the *Big Book* is the chapter, "There is a Solution." Wilson explains the essence of the "spiritual experience" when he recounts the conversation between "a certain American business man" and Dr. Carl Jung (Alcoholics Anonymous World Services 2001, 26). The businessman was Roland Hazard who later became active in the Oxford Group and mentored Ebby Thatcher, Wilson's original sponsor. According to Jung, lasting sobriety, as is true of any conversion, requires a spiritual experience "in the nature of huge emotional displacements and rearrangements. Ideas, emotions, and attitudes which were once the guiding forces of the lives of these men are suddenly cast to one side, and a completely new set of conceptions and motives begin to dominate them" (Alcoholics Anonymous World Services 2001, 27).

Edward Blackwell of Cornwall, N.Y. served as publisher of the *Big Book* in 1939. Wilson's physician from Towns Hospital, William Duncan Silkworth, wrote the introduction titled "The Doctor's Opinion." This introduction and the first one hundred sixty-four pages of text have remained unchanged ever since, with two exceptions. First, Silkworth's name was withheld from the first printing, possibly because of the controversial nature of the subject. Second, some readers of the first printing apparently felt that the spiritual experience described by Wilson had to be in the nature of "sudden and spectacular upheavals" (Alcoholics Anonymous World Services 2001, 567). As a consequence, in subsequent printings the wording of the Twelfth Step was changed from "spiritual experience" to "spiritual awakening," and an Appendix II was added to clarify that spiritual experience may be of the "'educational variety' . . . [that can] develop slowly over a period of time" (Alcoholics Anonymous World Services 2001, 567). Years later, Fr. Ed Dowling, SJ, unofficial sponsor to Bill W., continued to lament this change in wording. In an appeal to open-mindedness, Appendix II concludes with this quotation attributed to Herbert Spencer, but which may have originated with philosopher William Paley a century earlier: "There is a principle which is a bar against all information, which is proof against all arguments and which cannot fail to keep a man in everlasting ignorance—that principle is contempt prior to investigation" (Alcoholics Anonymous World Services 2001, 568).

Otherwise, the book *Alcoholics Anonymous* remained unchanged until 1955, when the second edition was published. The first one hundred sixty-four pages remained the same, but individual stories, which make up the second half of the book, were changed to better represent members of the time, and the Twelve Traditions were included. In 1976, the third edition of the *Big Book* appeared with the first half of the book intact, but with individual stories modified to reflect current membership, including stories by more women and more young members. Finally, in 2001 the fourth edition was introduced, again with only the personal stories modified to represent current membership in a virtual world.[3]

An interesting aspect of the *Big Book* is one of the individual stories by Dr. Paul Oligher. It appeared in the third edition under the title "Doctor, Alcoholic, Addict," and was renamed in the fourth edition to "Acceptance is the Answer," in part to avoid the emphasis upon drug addiction. A line that Dr. Paul is known for is, "And acceptance is the answer to *all* of my problems today" (Alcoholics Anonymous World Services 2001, 417; italics his). That celebrated line was on page 449 in the third edition, and was relocated to page 417 in the fourth edition. Dr. Paul's emphasis is helpful to many, but is theologically incomplete. It stresses the first part of the Serenity Prayer, "Accept the things I cannot change," and neglects the second part of "Courage to change the things I can."

Another significant story in the second half of the *Big Book* is "Doctor Bob's Nightmare." It is the one major part of A.A. literature that was written by the co-founder; it has consistently appeared in every edition of the *Big Book*, and is always the first story beginning on page 171. Dr. Bob tells his story, including why he helped over five thousand other alcoholics achieve sobriety without any financial compensation:

1. Sense of duty.

---

3. Alcoholics Anonymous General Services Inc. failed to renew its copyright on the first edition of the Big Book in 1967 and on the second edition in 1983. As A.A. acknowledges, "The First and Second Editions of the Big Book, Alcoholics Anonymous, are in the public domain in the United States *only*" (Alcoholics Anonymous World Services 2016, accessed December 2016; italics theirs). As a result, The Anonymous Press Inc. of Mato, WA also began printing and distributing copies of the Big Book.

Issues from Related Contemporary Literature

2. It is a pleasure.

3. Because in so doing I am paying my debt to the man who took time to pass it on to me.

4. Because every time I do it I take out a little more insurance for myself against a possible slip. (Alcoholics Anonymous World Services 2001, 181)

Enlarging on principles of the Oxford Group, *Alcoholics Anonymous* reflected the idea of a Christian deity and openly acknowledged ties to Christian churches. Finding the power of God is "exactly what this book is about" (Alcoholics Anonymous World Services 2001, 45). Personal stories, which comprise the second half of the book, describe how each individual "established his relationship with God" (Alcoholics Anonymous World Services 2001, 29). Passages such as the following reflect appreciation for established religions:

> We think it no concern of ours what religious bodies our members identify themselves with as individuals. This should be an entirely personal affair which each one decides for himself in the light of past associations, or his present choice. Not all of us join religious bodies, but most of us favor such memberships. (Alcoholics Anonymous World Services 2001, 28)

The book also affirms the importance of daily devotionals and the role of clergy:

> If we belong to a religious denomination which requires a definite morning devotion, we attend to that also. If not members of religious bodies, we sometimes select and memorize a few set prayers which emphasize the principles we have been discussing. There are many helpful books also. Suggestions about these may be obtained from one's priest, minister, or rabbi. Be quick to see where religious people are right. Make use of what they offer. (Alcoholics Anonymous World Services 2001, 87)

In *Alcoholics Anonymous*, the Twelve Steps appeared for the first time. Saul Selby, Director of Clinical Operations at Hazelden, points out, "As we explore the history of the Steps we will find that their roots are biblical, developed by devout followers of Christ" (Selby 2000, 4). The writing of the Twelve Steps was not the effort of Bill Wilson alone, but was the product of discussion and compromise among many early members of A.A. Wilson favored a more God-centered and Christian emphasis, as did Fitz M., Paul

K., and many members from Akron. As David Sheff remarks, "Wilson's original draft of the Big Book [sic] was intensely religious" (Sheff 2013, 215). Liberal members such as Hank P. and Jimmy B. represented atheists and agnostics who wanted the word "God" deleted altogether. The result was a compromise in which Wilson described God as a "*Power greater than ourselves*," and used the phrase, "God *as we understood Him*" (Alcoholics Anonymous World Services 2001, 45, 59; italics theirs). In Step Seven, he deleted the words, "on our knees" (Alcoholics Anonymous World Services 1984, 198), and he changed the introductory statement to say that the Steps were simply "suggested as a program of recovery" (Alcoholics Anonymous World Services 2001, 59). The outcome produced a program with the broadest possible appeal. As Wilson observes, "Countless A.A.'s have since testified that without this great evidence of liberality they never could have set foot on any path of spiritual progress or even approached us in the first place" (Alcoholics Anonymous World Services 1957, 167). The *Big Book* is one of the most published and influential books in the world next to the Bible. It is read and studied by millions of people.

The term "sponsor" is not used in the *Big Book*, and is not found in the earliest days of A.A. Apparently the concept originated when some hospitals in Akron and New York accepted alcoholic patients only if a member of Alcoholics Anonymous would accompany and support them. The sponsor checked the patient into the hospital, visited regularly, took them home on discharge, introduced them to A.A. meetings, and showed them how to work the program of Alcoholics Anonymous. The growth of A.A. was most dramatic in Cleveland under the leadership of Clarence Snyder, where sponsorship became commonplace. There are striking similarities between the A.A. sponsorship relationship and the Christian practice of spiritual mentoring, as between Paul and Timothy. One A.A. member speaks of having had a wonderful sponsor who was relatively uneducated but wise, had an incredible memory, and was a skillful listener. This individual remarks "Today I feel that sponsorship is the most important part of . . . [the] AA [sic] program. I believe that sponsorship is how AA [sic] was born. To me the story of Bill W. and Dr. Bob is a legacy of sponsorship at its best" (Terry H. 1994, 7).

An A.A. member of long standing sponsored hundreds of men recovering from addiction. An integral part of his sponsorship was "working the Steps" with newcomers. Typically a one-on-one activity, this can be done using a variety of resources including the *Twelve Steps and Twelve*

Issues from Related Contemporary Literature

Traditions, literature from Hazelton, and the *Big Book* itself. He prefers to use the original *Big Book* (Alcoholics Anonymous World Services 2001).

He meets newcomers five or more times for an hour or two on each occasion. Alternating the reading of pages, they read the chapters aloud, raise questions, discussing ideas as they go along, with the completion of the step marked by a handshake or a hug. At the first meeting, they read Chapter Two, "There is a Solution," which contains an introduction to both Step One and Step Two. They also read Chapter Three, "More About Alcoholism," and then take Step One. The second meeting they read Chapter Four, "We Agnostics," and take Step Two. At the second meeting they also read the beginning of Chapter Five, "How It Works," and take Step Three (including the Third Step prayer). The third meeting they read the balance of Chapter Five and assign Step Four, the personal inventory. The fourth meeting they discuss Step Four and complete Step Five. The fifth meeting they read Chapter Six, "Into Action," and take Steps Six and Seven (including the Seventh Step prayer). They assign Step Eight, which is making an amends list. The sixth meeting they review how the Ninth Step will be completed. They read Chapter Seven, "Working With Others," and discuss how Steps Ten, Eleven, and Twelve will be conducted. This schedule is flexible, and sometimes additional meetings are needed. An article in the *AA Grapevine* inspired this format:

> Monday came. After having breakfast, he [my sponsor] led me through the book and all the Steps in the next day and a half. He answered all my questions. We knelt and prayed at Steps Three and Seven. I did my inventory right out of the book. He never broke confidence in the things I shared from the Fifth Step. We worked out ways and means for me to make my amends. He explained Steps Ten, Eleven, and Twelve as the maintenance Steps. He told me that I was required to pass what I had learned on to other alcoholics. (Dave C. 2000, 11)

By the late twentieth century, clergy had become so accustomed to the Twelve Step ethos, that several articles were forthcoming that give guidance to clergy on how to help individuals complete the Fifth Step. Gregory P. Gabriel's study of "How Do You Hear a Fifth Step?" (Gabriel 1995, 97–115) and Mark A. Latcovich's article on "The Clergyperson and the Fifth Step" (Latcovich 1995, 79–89), both offer guidelines for ministers listening to the Fourth Step inventory by Twelve Step members. Sometimes done with one's sponsor, Fifth Steps may also be done with someone outside of the program for added expertise and for the assurance of confidentiality. Doing the Fifth

Step is a form of self-reporting and is not the same as a "confession," although one listens "to the other person in the name of God or a Higher Power" (Gabriel 1995, 100). As Latcovich explains, this process involves traditional Christian aspects of repentance, confession, and reconciliation with a soul-friend (Latcovich 1995, 80). The Fifth Step is telling one's "life story," a self-confession and a chance to leave behind one's mistakes. It should be completely confidential.

Being a partner in a Fifth Step does not mean trying to "fix" the person's problems, but simply listening carefully to them. Being able to listen and be a silent partner is vital. An hour and a half is not an unusual time frame; allowing two hours is a good idea. Revealing something of yourself can be a step in establishing a connection or friendship; it is not a clergyperson's job to evaluate. It is important to remember that people who self-disclose in the Fifth Step generally make themselves quite vulnerable. Latcovich remarks, "Being gentle with one's self during the Fifth Step process is an important and positive quality" (Latcovich 1995, 86). Confrontation or judgment is not the norm, but self-confrontation and acceptance are. It is vital to remember that alcoholics are people who judge themselves harshly, and feelings of guilt and remorse are frequently part of what is shared. "Negative feelings need to be shared and accepted before positive ones can fill their place" (Latcovich 1995, 87). It is important that pastors who listen to Fifth Steps are open to the process and comfortable with individuals recovering from addiction. Those taking the Fifth Step should be able to talk openly and without being judged. The pastor may ask about the individual's image of God, however, and may "need to re-present who God is . . . [with an emphasis on] God's mercy, compassion, forgiveness and power to save" (Latcovich 1995, 87). The minister might offer to pray with the person, and the person may be invited to rejoin his faith community. In short, the Fifth Step is when "A.A. shakes hands with religion—and one human being has made peace with God" (Gabriel 1995, 113). It is a commentary on how commonplace the Twelve Steps are that articles have appeared directed to people outside of A.A. who might be in a position to render assistance. These articles on participating in Fifth Steps should be included in the proposed syllabus.

Issues from Related Contemporary Literature

Other A.A. Literature

In the decade after the publication of the *Big Book*, A.A. members felt the need for a more detailed narrative of the Twelve Steps. Furthermore, as the group underwent growing pains, the pressure grew on Wilson to provide organizational guidelines. In 1952, Wilson was also the chief writer of *Twelve Steps and Twelve Traditions* (Alcoholics Anonymous World Services 2011), but availed himself of the collaboration of a panel of journalists including Tom Powers, Betty Love, and Jack Alexander. Coming thirteen years after *Alcoholics Anonymous* was first published, *Twelve Steps and Twelve Traditions* was in effect "A.A.'s New Testament—bringing to fruition the original revelation of the Big Book" (Kurtz 1991, 124). This second foundational document of A.A. introduces organizational principles known as the "Twelve Traditions," and adds more depth to the conversation about the Steps.

The Twelve Traditions are as follows:

1. Our common welfare should come first; personal recovery depends upon A.A. unity.
2. For our group purpose there is but one ultimate authority—a loving God as He may express Himself in our group conscience. Our leaders are but trusted servants; they do not govern.
3. The only requirement for A.A. membership is a desire to stop drinking.
4. Each group should be autonomous except in matters affecting other groups or A.A. as a whole.
5. Each group has but one primary purpose—to carry its message to the alcoholic who still suffers.
6. An A.A. group ought never endorse, finance, or lend the A.A. name to any related facility or outside enterprise, lest problems of money, property, and prestige divert us from our primary purpose.
7. Every A.A. group ought to be fully self-supporting, declining outside contributions.
8. Alcoholics Anonymous should remain forever nonprofessional, but our service centers may employ special workers.
9. A.A., as such, ought never be organized; but we may create service boards or committees directly responsible to those they serve.

10. Alcoholics Anonymous has no opinion on outside issues; hence the A.A. name ought never be drawn into public controversy.

11. Our public relations policy is based on attraction rather than promotion; we need always maintain personal anonymity at the level of press, radio, and films.

12. Anonymity is the spiritual foundation of all our traditions, ever reminding us to place principles before personalities (Alcoholics Anonymous World Services 2011, 9–13. Reprinted with permission of Alcoholics Anonymous World Services Inc.)

One of the best examples of adding depth to the conversation about the Steps in *Twelve Steps and Twelve Traditions* is the discussion by the authors of personal relationships. It must be remembered that the writing is no longer Wilson's alone—nor are some of the insights. In the chapter on Step Four, the authors comment:

> But it is from our twisted relations with family, friends, and society at large that many of us have suffered the most.... we fail to recognize ... our total inability to form a true partnership with another human being.... Either we insist upon dominating the people we know, or we depend upon them far too much. (Alcoholics Anonymous World Services 2011, 53)

This theme is renewed and amplified in the chapter on Step Twelve. As the authors observe, we were "constantly thrown ... into unworkable relations with other people" (Alcoholics Anonymous World Services 2011, 115). We ran to extremes, "Either we had tried to play God and dominate those about us, or we had insisted on being overdependent upon them" (Alcoholics Anonymous World Services 2011, 115). If we wanted to feel emotionally secure, "we would have to put our lives on a give-and-take basis; we would have to develop the sense of being in partnership or brotherhood with all those around us" (Alcoholics Anonymous World Services 2011, 116). The writers present a strong argument for believing in God: "If we really depended upon God, we couldn't very well play God to our fellows nor would we feel the urge wholly to rely on human protection and care" (Alcoholics Anonymous World Services 2011, 116). This researcher finds that *Twelve Steps and Twelve Traditions* is sometimes quite insightful and eloquent.

In addition, Wilson and other recovering alcoholics realized the need for a small book of daily devotions, but lacked the energy or inclination for it. Filling this gap, Richmond Walker from Boston published his little book, *Twenty-Four Hours a Day* (Walker 2013), a volume of daily meditations and prayers that took A.A. members by storm in 1948. Approximately half of the A.A.'s in the United States owned a copy of Walker's volume. In 1954, the Hazelden Foundation, a treatment center in Minnesota, "offered to take over the task of printing and distributing the books" (Dubiel 2004, 133). "Five thousand copies were sold when the book was released in 1954, eighty thousand by 1959, seven million by 1990, and well over 8.2 million as of 2013. Including translated editions, worldwide sales to date exceed 9.7 million" (Walker 2013, Foreword). *Twenty-Four Hours a Day* drew heavily from the book *Alcoholics Anonymous,* from Emmet Fox, and from the Oxford Group, but its overall tone is "closer to the teachings of the Emmanuel Movement and the Jacoby Club than it is to that of the Oxford Group" (Dubiel 2004, 134). Members accepted this little black book as the primary meditation book until A.A. finally published its own *Daily Reflections* (Alcoholics Anonymous World Services 1990).

A.A. also published a volume of excerpts from writings and letters of Wilson titled *The A.A. Way of Life: . . .Selected Writings of A.A.'s Co-Founder* (Alcoholics Anonymous World Services 1967), and subsequently renamed *As Bill Sees It: The A.A. Way of Life.* Likewise, excerpts of Wilson's articles from the A.A. monthly journal, the *AA Grapevine,* were collected and published under the title *The Language of the Heart* (Wilson 2011). These auxiliary manuals are designed to supplement the *Big Book,* and both books serve as an invaluable source of topics for A.A. meetings. Finally, *Living Sober* (Alcoholics Anonymous World Services 1975b) offers sound practical advice for newcomers in A.A. It presents the fundamentals of the program in the simplest terms, and is a viable resource for the alcoholic who is still befogged. The practical advice it offers ranges on topics as diverse as the "24-hour Plan," using the Serenity Prayer, "Telephone Therapy," fending off loneliness, and seeking professional help.

The Curriculum of Celebrate Recovery

A notable exception to the primacy of A.A. is Celebrate Recovery (C.R.), founded by John Baker and Rick Warren. These authors offer a contrasting voice in the conversation on Twelve Step philosophy. Baker and Warren disclose how the Twelve Steps function in a Christ-centered context, and include four primary texts: *Stepping Out of Denial Into God's Grace* (Baker 2012a); *Taking an Honest and Spiritual Inventory* (Baker 2012b); *Getting Right with God, Yourself, and Others* (Baker 2012c); and *Growing in Christ While Helping Others* (Baker 2012d). The chief contrast of the publications of Celebrate Recovery is the recognition of Jesus Christ as the Higher Power. Its publications are as important to study as the *Big Book* for those concerned with the Twelve Step process.

Celebrate Recovery was founded in 1990 at the Saddleback Church in Lake Forest, California. John Baker wrote Pastor Rick Warren a thirteen-page, single-spaced letter "outlining the vision God had given him for Celebrate Recovery. After reading John's letter, Pastor Rick said, 'Great John, go do it!' The first night forty-five people attended, and Celebrate Recovery was born" (Green Acres Baptist Church n.d., accessed September 2016). Since then, over ten thousand people have participated in the program at the Saddleback Church. Today, more than twenty-nine thousand churches use the Celebrate Recovery curriculum in fifty states and twenty-five foreign countries, and a total of one million people have worked this program. Celebrate Recovery utilizes the Twelve Steps of A.A., with the First Step modified to include other addictions and compulsive behaviors. In addition, the following biblical comparisons are added to each of the Steps:

1. We admitted we were powerless over our addictions and compulsive behaviors, that our lives had become unmanageable. "I know that nothing good lives in me, that is, in my sinful nature. For I have the desire to do what is good, but I cannot carry it out" (Rom 7:18).

2. We came to believe that a power greater than ourselves could restore us to sanity. "For it is God who works in you to will and to act according to his good purpose" (Phil 2:1).

3. We made a decision to turn our lives and our wills over to the care of God. "Therefore, I urge you, brothers, in view of God's mercy, to offer your bodies as living sacrifices, holy and pleasing to God—this is your spiritual act of worship" (Rom 12:1).

4. We made a searching and fearless moral inventory of ourselves. "Let us examine our ways and test them, and let us return to the Lord" (Lam 3:40).

Issues from Related Contemporary Literature

5. We admitted to God, to ourselves, and to another human being the exact nature of our wrongs. "Therefore confess your sins to each other and pray for each other so that you may be healed" (Jas 5:16).

6. We were entirely ready to have God remove all these defects of character. "Humble yourselves before the Lord, and he will lift you up" (Jas 4:10).

7. We humbly asked Him to remove all our shortcomings. "If we confess our sins, he is faithful and will forgive us our sins and purify us from all unrighteousness" (1 John 1:9).

8. We made a list of all persons we had harmed and became willing to make amends to them all. "Do to others as you would have them do to you" (Luke 6:31).

9. We made direct amends to such people whenever possible, except when to do so would injure them or others. "Therefore, if you are offering your gift at the altar and there remember that your brother has something against you, leave your gift there in front of the altar. First go and be reconciled to your brother; then come and offer your gift" (Matt 5:23–24).

10. We continue to take personal inventory and when we were wrong, promptly admitted it. "So, if you think you are standing firm, be careful that you don't fall!" (1 Cor 10:12).

11. We sought through prayer and meditation to improve our conscious contact with God, praying only for knowledge of His will for us, and power to carry that out. "Let the word of Christ dwell in you richly" (Col 3:16).

12. Having had a spiritual experience as the result of these steps, we try to carry this message to others and practice these principles in all our affairs. "Brothers, if someone is caught in a sin, you who are spiritual should restore them gently. But watch yourself, or you also may be tempted" (Gal 6:1). (Celebrate Recovery 2015a, accessed July 2017. Reprinted with permission of Celebrate Recovery.)

Furthermore, Celebrate Recovery has Eight Principles, which are based upon Christ's Beatitudes:

1. Realize I'm not God; I admit that I am powerless to control my tendency to do the wrong thing and that my life is unmanageable (Step 1). *"Happy are those who know that they are spiritually poor."*
2. Earnestly believe that God exists, that I matter to Him and that He has the power to help me recover (Step 2). *"Happy are those who mourn, for they shall be comforted."*
3. Consciously choose to commit all my life and will to Christ's care and control (Step 3). *"Happy are the meek."*
4. Openly examine and confess my faults to myself, to God, and to someone I trust (Steps 4 and 5). *"Happy are the pure in heart."*
5. Voluntarily submit to any and all changes God wants to make in my life and humbly ask Him to remove my character defects (Steps 6 and 7). *"Happy are those whose greatest desire is to do what God requires."*
6. Evaluate all my relationships. Offer forgiveness to those who have hurt me and make amends for harm I've done to others when possible, except when to do so would harm them or others (Steps 8 and 9). *"Happy are the merciful." "Happy are the peacemakers."*
7. Reserve a time with God for self-examination, Bible reading, and prayer in order to know God and His will for my life and to gain the power to follow His will (Steps 10 and 11).
8. Yield myself to God to be used to bring this Good News to others, both by my example and my words (Step 12). *"Happy are those who are persecuted because they do what God requires."* (Celebrate Recovery 2015b, accessed July 2017; italics theirs. Reprinted with permission of Celebrate Recovery.)

In January 2014, this researcher attended a weekend Celebrate Recovery retreat at Grace United Methodist Church in Fort Myers, Florida. Under the pastorate of Jorge Acevedo, Grace Church has five campuses in Southwest Florida—Cape Coral, Fort Myers Shores, Fort Myers Central, Fort Myers Trinity and Sarasota. Grace Church has grown in weekend attendance from four hundred to over two thousand six hundred in the past nineteen years, and has one of the largest and most effective recovery ministries in America, emphasizing recovery from anger, chemical dependency, codependency, abuse, sexual addiction, and love and relationship addiction. As Acevedo observes, "Many churches . . . offer people Jesus the Healer without offering healing ministries" (Swanson and McBean 2011,

109). Clearly, Christ-centered programs such as Celebrate Recovery are a significant aspect of the Twelve Step movement.

An Alternative View of the Disease Concept And the Twelve Steps

In the dialogue taking place on the Twelve Steps, there are authors who are critical of the disease model and how Twelve Step organizations work. Herbert Fingarette's book, *Heavy Drinking: The Myth of Alcoholism as a Disease* (Fingarette 1988), argues that addiction as a disease is a fiction and that heavy drinkers can be helped to regain control. A few years later Stanton Peele published his study, *Diseasing of America: How We Allowed Recovery Zealots and the Treatment Industry to Convince Us We Are Out of Control* (Peele 1995), in which he contends that addiction is not a disease and that the treatment industry is unnecessary because "people will get better over time, usually on their own" (Peele 1995, 176). William L. Playfair's book, *The Useful Lie*, is a classic statement of this position, dealing with the "mistreatment industry," the "diseasing of Christianity," the "failure of the recovery industry," and the "myth of Christian origins" of A.A. (Playfair 1991, 21, 25, 62, 86). Also in 1991, Martin and Deidre Bobgan published their work, *12 Steps to Destruction: Codependency Recovery Heresies*, in which they find the Twelve Steps are "no different from any other moralistic or religious plan for self-improvement" and that there is "no clear etiology for the disease" concept of alcoholism (Bobgan 1991, 205, 74).

In a similar vein, J. B. Myers published his volume, *Faith and Addiction: A Faith Alternative to the Twelve Steps Theory and Disease Mode of Addiction Treatment* (Myers 2007), in which he recommends "an alternative that is both biblically based and more effective than what is currently presented to religious people" (Myers 2007, Introduction). He disputes the disease concept of addiction, argues against the Twelve Steps as an example of "groupthink," disputes whether drugs cause addiction, and proposes that to stop addictive behavior such as gambling the addict simply needs to "exercise your willpower" (Myers 2007, 102). Although clearly a minority view, literature expressing an alternative perspective of the disease concept and the Twelve Steps should be acknowledged. Perhaps there would be reason for suspicion if there was no recognition of such dissenting voices.

LITERATURE ON THE SPIRITUAL FEATURES OF THE TWELVE STEP DESIGN AND ITS RELATION TO CHRISTIANITY

In the development of a syllabus for clergy and those in ministerial training, another issue is the spiritual aspect of the Twelve Steps and its influence on Christian ministry. Numerous sources discuss the impact of the Twelve Steps on ministry. Some sources give acclaim to A.A., as does Dennis C. Morreim who confirms in his book, *The Road to Recovery*, that "The theme of spiritual change (conversion) through the grace of God emerges repeatedly throughout the literature of AA [sic]" (Morreim 1990, 54–55). He emphasizes the similarity between A.A. and churches:

> AA [sic] and the church are parallel roads, traveling the same direction, covering similar terrain, yet consistently maintaining their distance. . . . Though there are differences in these parallel roads, there are places along the way where both AA and the Christian church have some common ground. . . . Both AA and the church proclaim the grace of God. (Morreim 1990, 132–33)

Likewise, Michele S. Matto gives an enthusiastic endorsement of A.A.: "We who are in Twelve Step programs are a group of people who have already been brought to our knees by life's circumstances. . . . The Twelve Steps are nothing more and nothing less than what the church has been about all these centuries" (Matto 1991, 9). John E. Keller adds a caveat to this conversation, as he says in his study, *Ministering to Alcoholics*: "A.A. tells us just what the church has been saying for years. The alcoholic is powerless over alcohol, and his hope is ultimately in God. But A.A. recognizes that, while the alcoholic surely needs God, he just as surely does not need moralism" (Keller 1966, 1). J. Keith Miller offers this testimonial from his book, *A Hunger for Healing*: "My experience in Twelve-Step groups has convinced me that God has provided a way of spiritual healing and growth that may well be the most important spiritual model of any age for contemporary Christians" (Miller 1991, xii). Morreim, Matto, Keller, and J. Keith Miller give compelling testimony from the perspective of Christian ministry on the spiritual features of the Twelve Steps and their relationship to Christianity.

Specific Spiritual Features of the Twelve Steps

In this discussion, some writers address specific spiritual features of the Twelve Step design. Charles T. Knippel examines theological issues in his book, *The 12 Steps: The Church's Challenge and Opportunity* (Knippel 1994). He emphasizes the natural knowledge of God through his creative work, because it is written in human hearts and because it works in nature and history. Knippel concludes:

> Persuasive biblical reasons compel us to believe that God uses the Twelve Step Program to empower people to recover from addictions.... The benefits of the Twelve Steps come to people through their natural knowledge of God and their capacity to respond with outward good works. God works in the secular sphere as well as in the spiritual, rules with His left hand as well as His right. (Knippel 1994, 69)

Continuing this dialogue, John F. Woolverton remarks in his article, "Evangelical Protestantism and Alcoholism 1933–1962:"

> As for A.A., it never had a chance to develop a resonant theology because it was never offered one. That it did not wholly lose a sense of the transcendent power of God or fold it entirely into an Immanence which would become simply the communal mind of the group is to its credit. Indeed, something of a miracle. (Woolverton 1983, 163)

Ernest Kurtz changes hats from historian to mystic in co-authoring a book with Katherine Ketcham titled, *The Spirituality of Imperfection: Storytelling and the Search for Meaning* (Kurtz and Ketcham 2002). This book highlights various stories reflecting spirituality's qualities of freedom, gratitude, humility, honesty, and forgiveness.

Michael Hardin responds on the issue of spirituality with his article, "The Twelve Step Program and Christian Spirituality," saying that "The Twelve Steps share a dual focus also found in certain Christian traditions, viz., that the knowledge of God and knowledge of ourselves is intertwined" (Hardin 1994a, 48), and that "There is in the Christian tradition ample reason to accept the paradigm of spirituality found in the Twelve Step tradition" (Hardin 1994a, 55). He sees the Twelve Steps as an application of Christian spirituality, an example of the "purgation-illumination-union" model. He perceives that Steps One through Three are the first stage of purgation; the second stage of illumination is reflected in Steps Four through Ten; and the third stage of union is achieved in Steps Eleven and Twelve.

Michael Hardin's article, "Let God be God: A Theological Justification for the Anonymity of God in the 12 Step Program" (Hardin 1994b, 9–22), makes a special contribution to the dialogue in his discussion of the identity of God in the Twelve Step paradigm. Although little has been written from a Christian viewpoint that justifies the anonymity of God, he insists that "the God of the Bible is free, free from our theology and our theological models" (Hardin 1994b, 15). He argues that: "If one looks at the 12 Steps and 12 Traditions carefully one observes an amazing congruence between the gospel and anonymous spirituality. . . . However, others have sought to Christianize the 12 Steps without realizing the strategic importance of letting God remain anonymous" (Hardin 1994b, 19). Hardin concludes, "the anonymous God of the 12 Steps is the unknown God whom we can and may proclaim in our therapy, our preaching, and our teaching" (Hardin 1994b, 20). Michael Hardin's articles are insightful and illustrate what is written from a Christian perspective on the spiritual features of the Twelve Steps.

William McDonough contributes to this discussion in his article on "Sin and Addiction: Alcoholics Anonymous and the Soul of Christian Sin-Talk" (McDonough 2012, 39–55). He chronicles the use of the concept of sin in A.A. literature, beginning with the *Big Book* where Bill Wilson "gives this autobiographical account of his own alcoholism . . . 'I ruthlessly faced my sins and became willing to have my new-found Friend take them away, root and branch'" (McDonough 2012, 41). Wilson discusses the "Seven Deadly Sins" when considering moral inventory in the book, *Twelve Steps and Twelve Traditions* (McDonough 2012, 42). He studied the "capital sins" in *The Spiritual Exercises of St. Ignatius*, "given to him by Jesuit priest Ed Dowling" (McDonough 2012, 44). McDonough has proved to be a valued resource in discussing the spirituality of the Twelve Steps.

Several articles analyze the Twelve Steps from the standpoint of specific Protestant denominations. Sharon G. Kapsch gives "A Lutheran Reflection on the 'Twelve Steps of AA'" (Kapsch 1997, 53–67). She cites the evangelical mode of Steps Eight through Twelve that focus on transformation. After the spiritual awakening in Step Twelve, the good news is proclaimed to others with "missionary zeal" (Kapsch 1997, 57). Kapsch recommends that Alcoholics Anonymous literature be displayed in church offices, that pastors be available to hear Fifth Step disclosures, take an active role in interventions, discuss addiction from the pulpit, and facilitate Twelve Step groups in their churches.

The role of the Presbyterian Church in addiction recovery is encouraged by William R. Miller in his article, "Toward A Biblical Perspective on Drug Use" (Miller 1993, 77–85). Miller, who is a leading figure in the field of addiction and treatment, also has a background in theology. Consequently, he emphasizes the social policy on alcohol use and abuse in the Presbyterian Church since 1986. In a similar vein, Robin Crawford contributes to the discussion with his article, "The Presbyterian Church in the United States of America: A History of Concern for the Addictions" (Crawford 1997, 69–79). He recalls Benjamin Rush's presentation of copies of his treatise on excessive drinking to the Presbyterian General Assembly, and Presbyterianism's statements concerning alcohol beginning in 1812. The southern Presbyterian General Assembly called for banishing liquor in 1886, and the northern church did likewise in 1895. The Presbyterian Church was the largest denomination to accept the disease model of alcoholism in 1946, advocated tough laws about drinking and driving between 1947 and 1986, took strong stands on tobacco, illegal drugs, and behavior addictions such as gambling. It is a commentary on the social acceptance of the Twelve Step philosophy that so many studies explore its relationship to major churches.

An Alternative View of the Spirituality of the Twelve Steps

Just as there is an alternative perspective on how the Twelve Steps work and the disease concept of alcoholism, there is an alternative view of the spiritual features of the Twelve Steps. Dissenting views on the spirituality of the Twelve Steps include those of Martin and Deidre Bobgan, William L. Playfair, David L. Simmons, and Paul R. Stark. The Bobgans give a classic statement of rejection of A.A.'s spirituality:

> Most systems of codependency and addiction recovery are based upon various psychological counseling theories and therapies and upon the religious and philosophical teachings of Alcoholics Anonymous (AA). In short, such programs are based upon the wisdom of man and the worship of false gods. . . . If Jesus is truly the answer to life's problems and indeed the very source of life, why are both nonChristians [sic] and Christians looking for answers elsewhere? (Bobgan 1991, 5, 7)

William L. Playfair also argues, "Rather than allow God's Word and wisdom to direct and shape the church's policies about addictive and destructive behaviors, many are content merely to rely upon the recovery industry" (Playfair 1991, 82). David L. Simmons, a disgruntled former A.A. member, states, "I now understand that recovery (applying the spiritual principles of the Alcoholics Anonymous program every moment) is lacking when it comes to my eternal state before God.... I can no longer endorse the AA message or its idolatrous teachings" (Simmons 2012, 5, 82). For a critique of Celebrate Recovery, see Paul R. Stark: "Participants are considered 'in recovery,' rather than 'in Christ,' thereby perpetuating the disease myth and lifelong enslavement to the pretension that addiction is chronic" (Stark 2004, 11, accessed May 2015).

Linda A. Mercadante: A Theological Perspective

Linda Mercadante of the Methodist Theological School in Ohio is one of today's most prolific writers on the subject of theology and addiction. Her writings represent "contemporary Christian ethics' most sustained attempt to understand AA" (McDonough 2012, 40). She has authored five or more books, contributed to many others, and written more than fifty articles on the subjects of theology, addiction, and gender. She makes a major contribution to the dialogue on A.A.'s relationship to Christianity, and some of her works are included in this study.

Mercadante considers addiction and Twelve Step philosophy from the vantage point of theology in her classic work, *Victims & Sinners: Spiritual Roots of Addiction and Recovery* (Mercadante 1996a). As she reflects, the addiction recovery process is said to be "spiritual but not religious," although much of it comes from Christianity (Mercadante 1966a, ix). She is an advocate of collaboration between religion and addiction treatment:

> The church has had thousands of years to ponder the human condition, its potential and its difficulties. To dismiss this experience out of hand is obviously shortsighted. Likewise, those employed in the field of addiction treatment and research have spent much time working to free persons from this bondage.... To turn one's back on this practical pedagogy is counterproductive. (Mercadante 1996a, 14)

Comparing sin to addiction, she reviews the view of Pelagius who declared that people exercise free will, and the perspective of Augustine who believed in the power of transmitted sin, yet saw the voluntary element and held that humans were responsible. She continues, "AA's [sic] claim that one is powerless over alcohol . . . is a distinct challenge to this Pelagian mind-set. In fact, the argument sounds something like Augustine's. This gives the AA [sic] message persuasive power both in and out of the church" (Mercadante 1996a, 116). She conceives of sin as disorder, disinclination or disorientation, and she defines it as "primarily a turning from the source of our being, God" (Mercadante 1996a, 35). Both themes of sin and conversion became a part of the A.A. model. She remarks that, "The idea of addiction as physical is as close as the modern mind may come to a descriptive picture of original sin, especially when genetics or inherited characteristics are stressed" (Mercadante 1996a, 115), and she concludes her book with this reflection:

> The Oxford Group worked for the revitalization of the world's morality. The recovery program limits its sights to individual restoration. Nevertheless, on a limited scale, it is a scenario of salvation. Most obviously, of course, in the minimalist AA [sic] version there is no Christ figure, no objective act of redemption done for humankind, no concern for eternal life, no divine plan for the world, no cosmology to situate evil and good. (Mercadante 1996a, 164)

Her article, "The Religious and Theological Roots of Alcoholics Anonymous," expands the sin-versus-disease dichotomy by considering further the Pelagian and Augustinian views of sin (Mercadante 2009, 98–105). However, her article titled "Sin, Gender, and Addiction" (Mercadante 1997, 37–45) is one of the best expositions of her concept of sin in the addiction model. She places great emphasis on what sin is not—the condemnation of particular acts, and the separation of sinners from the saved. As previously quoted, "Sin is not primarily about behavior, morality, nor acts. Instead it is about one's primary orientation, telos, direction" (Mercadante 1997, 39). She defines sin as "turning away from God and the good" (Mercadante 1997, 38). She argues that increasingly troublesome behavior falls into the category of disease, yet A.A. could not take an entirely medical approach because it originated in the Oxford Group which stressed sin and conversion. A.A. tried to deal with this by minimizing religious terms, which helped get people in the front door. This, however, became a problem when churches integrated recovery models in their institutions, or referred addicted members to outside Twelve Step programs. Mercadante maintains that the generic spirituality of the Twelve Step model has discarded too much, specifically the nature of God, Christology, the role of grace, a future life, and a doctrine of the church. The spirituality of the Twelve Steps is in "need of serious supplementation and theological correction when it is brought into the church or other religious settings, or when it begins to function as one's primary spirituality" (Mercadante 1997, 44). Ultimately, the model gained in recovery

> does not always replicate the deepest, or best, theological understanding of sin as human dysfunction. . . . AA [sic] and related groups did not want to replicate religion—they wanted to help addicts. But the recovery process has become the primary spirituality for hundreds of thousands, maybe millions, of people. It was never meant to be that. Even Bill Wilson said AA [sic] was just a spiritual kindergarten. (Mercadante 1997, 43)

Perhaps the most informative article by Mercadante on A.A.'s relationship to Christian theology is "Sin, Addiction, and Freedom," published in the volume, *Reconstructing Christian Theology* (Mercadante 1994, 220–44). She refers to the classic disease theory of addiction that gained traction after Prohibition when drinking moved increasingly from choice to compulsion. She suggests that the reason for the use of the disease concept of addiction, instead of that of sin, stems from

> a cultural rejection of the concept of sin, especially when that concept is understood as harsh, judgmental, punitive, and pessimistic. To say an addict or alcoholic is sick rather than sinful is today deemed more compassionate, relieving guilt feelings, giving hope of improvement, calling for sympathy rather than condemnation. (Mercadante 1994, 226–27)

She considers if the concept of addiction is simply a modern way of dealing with sin. The trap of addiction may simply be the latest face of a centuries-old adversary. In her article, Mercadante proceeds to outline the history and diversity of the concept of sin, and anticipates some observations in her book. She discusses the Manichean version, which was unduly pessimistic and perceived sin and finitude as synonymous, while the Pelagian version conceived of sin as making an avoidable mistake. The Augustinian doctrine is seen as the "self-imposed bondage of the will" (Mercadante 1994, 229). In short, the doctrine of sin balances human responsibility and freedom against the forces of evil. As she says, "we have too long stressed the power and independence of the will. Indeed, much of North American theology has had a Pelagian cast" (Mercadante 1994, 233).

On one hand, A.A. is Manichean, referring to the inherency of disease, and at the same time Pelagian in its optimism for those suffering from a treatable condition.

Thus, sin and addiction have much in common. Both concepts address the human predicament of not being able to do the good. Further, there are parallels between addiction and a worldly view of original sin. Mercadante concludes her part in the dialogue about the relationship of recovery to Christianity, "In many ways sin really is like addiction, partly inherited, partly chosen, easy to get into, difficult to get out of. . . . The recovery movement, for all its attention to addiction, does hold out hope for despairing people. The church must be recalled to its task of doing no less" (Mercadante 1994, 239–40).

As is true of Kurtz, Linda Mercadante occupies a position of academic credibility and depth of scholarship. Her commentary on sin and addiction is unique and provides an invaluable contribution to this study. The current writer acknowledges his limitations as a theologian, and looks forward to future discussion on sin and addiction, as well as on grace and recovery.

The Heritage of Howard J. Clinebell Jr. and Robert H. Albers

Another voice contributing to the discussion about Christianity embracing the Twelve Steps and incorporating them into pastoral care is that of Howard J. Clinebell Jr. His book, *Understanding and Counseling the Alcoholic: Through Religion and Psychology* (Clinebell 1956b), set the tone for discussion between Twelve Step proponents and Christianity. His book was significantly updated in 1968 and in 1998. Clinebell exhaustively considered the causes of alcoholism and surveyed Christian-based approaches including the Emmanuel Movement and Alcoholics Anonymous. He developed guidelines for the minister's counseling role of the alcoholic, helping families who are affected, and strategies for the congregation in supporting the recovering alcoholic. Clinebell was a mentor to Robert H. Albers, who continued discussion of Christian ministry in addiction recovery as an educator and editor. Significantly, Albers also wrote a curriculum, *Addiction and the Family: A Seminary Curriculum* (Albers 2012), published by the National Association for Children of Alcoholics. Ideal for self-study, the core competencies addressed in this curriculum are attitudes, awareness, assimilation, and action. Unit downloads are available online, or it may be purchased from NACOA at a nominal charge.

Albers also served as editor of the *Journal of Ministry in Addiction & Recovery*. This specialized journal was published between 1994 and 2002 and provided a forum for dialogue between Christian leaders on addiction recovery issues. Throughout the years it was in print, articles appeared on such diverse topics as the following:

- Spirituality (Gabriel 1994, 41–46; Hardin 1994a, 47–68; Albers 1994, 47–69; Claytor 1998, 31–36; Sandoz 1999a, 99–107; Hart 1999, 25–39; Sandoz 1999b, 53–59)
- Anonymity of God (Hardin 1994b, 9–22)
- Drug use (Miller 1995, 77–85)
- Fifth Step (Gabriel 1995, 97–115)
- Jesus (Lee 1996, 17–32)
- Recovery (Albers 1997, 23–36)
- Sin (Mercadante 1997, 37–45)
- Theology (Lattimore 1997, 47–62)
- Lutheran Church (Kapsch 1997, 53–67)
- Presbyterian Church (Crawford 1997, 69–79)
- Bible (Michael 1998, 75–84)

Clinebell and Albers have contributed much to the relationship of Christian ministry to addiction recovery. A syllabus for ministers in training should honor that legacy.

The Views of Gerald G. May

Psychiatrist Gerald G. May adds another dimension to the conversation between recovery proponents and religion. He sets a new standard for the dialogue on the relationship of addiction with theology in his crossover work, *Addiction and Grace* (May 1991). His classic definition of addiction is "any compulsive, habitual behavior that limits the freedom of human desire. It is caused by the attachment, or nailing, of desire to specific objects" (May 1991, 24–25). Philip J. Flores takes the concept of attachment a step further in his volume *Addiction as an Attachment Disorder* (Flores 2004).

According to May, two forces turn us away from living life fully. Either we repress our desire for love to minimize vulnerability, or we may turn to addiction. May points out that, "While repression stifles desire, addiction *attaches* desire . . . to certain specific behaviors, things, or people" (May 1991, 3; italics his). He further explains that an "authentic faith can never become an attachment" and that "grace's empowerment is present in all true healings, in deliverances of all kinds" (May 1991, 130, 154). May is eminent as both a therapist and an author. Although unconventional in his approach to Christian theology, he sets a high bar in the discussion for those concerned with addiction and religion. May's work would provide a provocative, if unorthodox, voice in a syllabus for ministerial training.

General Reference Works

In the background of other authors talking to each other, Wayne Grudem's *Systematic Theology: An Introduction to Biblical Doctrine* (Grudem 1994), provides a general framework of theology. In addition, Paul Tillich's three volume *Systematic Theology* (Tillich 1967) speaks with authority in resolving many theological issues. In a similar vein, Sydney E. Ahlstrom's history, *A Religious History of the American People* (Ahlstrom 1973), provides a court of last appeal on historical questions such as the effect of Prohibition. In researching Dietrich Bonhoeffer's views of "unconscious Christianity," his *Letters and Papers From Prison* (Bonhoeffer 2015, 475) is indispensable. Finally, in exploring Karl Rahner's concept of the "Anonymous Christian," volume XIV of his *Theological Investigations* (Rahner 1976, 283) is crucial. These classic references provide the theme for this study and the context for a course syllabus on ministry and addiction recovery.

LITERATURE ON CURRENT INFORMATION ON ADDICTION THEORY

Another issue to understand in creating a syllabus for clergy and those in ministerial training is the status of addiction theory. Fortunately, there is an abundance of contemporary literature on this subject. For example, David Sheff's book, *Clean: Overcoming Addiction and Ending America's Greatest Tragedy* (Sheff 2013), gives an excellent overview of the problem of addiction. One of the leading contributors to the field of addiction is William R. Miller. He co-edited the texts *Re-thinking Substance Abuse: What the Science Shows, and What We Should Do About It* (Miller and Carroll 2006), *Research on Alcoholics Anonymous: Opportunities and Alternatives* (McCrady and Miller

1993), and he authored *Integrating Spirituality into Treatment: Resources for Practitioners* (Miller 2010). The first represents a basic text encompassing the range of addiction, while the last includes consideration of prayer, forgiveness, hope, serenity, and spirituality in general. Kathleen M. Carroll joins Miller in offering the following perspective on the hallmark questions that addiction raises:

> [T]he central issues of this field represent a microcosm of classic human dilemmas: why we persist in patterns of behavior that clearly lead toward devastating consequences; the tensions among our biological, individual, and social selves; whether and how to regulate our emotions; the trade-offs of immediate gratification versus long-term personal, family, and communal welfare. (Miller and Carroll 2006, 6)

Next, the current study utilized the American Psychiatric Association's *Diagnostic and Statistical Manual of Mental Disorders* (American Psychiatric Association 2013), better known as the *DSM-5*. It stresses that substance-related addictions "have in common direct activation of the brain reward system. . . . drugs of abuse directly activate the reward pathways" (American Psychiatric Association 2013, 481). The *DSM-5* differs from previous editions in the inclusion of behavioral addictions by adding gambling: "An important departure from past diagnostic manuals is that the chapter on substance-related disorders has been expanded to include *gambling disorder*" (American Psychiatric Association 2013, 815; italics theirs). The addition of other behavioral or process addictions is pending but has not yet occurred, because "at this time there is insufficient peer-reviewed evidence to establish the diagnostic criteria" (American Psychiatric Association 2013, 481).

This research also drew upon the fifth edition of *The ASAM Principles of Addiction Medicine* (Ries et al. 2014), published by the American Society of Addiction Medicine, formerly known as the American Society on Alcoholism and Other Drug Dependencies. In 1990, the ASAM had published this definition of alcoholism:

> Alcoholism is a primary, chronic *disease* with genetic, psychosocial, and environmental factors influencing its development and manifestations. The disease is often *progressive and fatal*. It is characterized by continuous or periodic: *Impaired* control over drinking, *preoccupation* with the drug alcohol, use of alcohol despite

adverse consequences, and distortions in thinking, most notably *denial*. (ASAM 2005, accessed January 2016; italics theirs)

The ASAM now emphasizes the neurobiological basis of addiction: "drug addiction is a disease of the brain and . . . the associated abnormal behaviors . . . are the result of dysfunctional brain tissue, just as cardiac insufficiency is a disease of the heart and abnormal blood circulation is the result of impaired myocardial function" (Volkow and Warren 2014, 3). The ASAM volume and the *DSM-5* are basic reference books for the treatment industry and establish the criteria for diagnosis and evaluation. They provide a level of sophistication and professionalism requisite for any course on addiction recovery.

The Evolutionary Roots of Addiction

One important concept—the benchmark of current discussion—is that addiction is a product of an evolutionary survival mechanism. Addictionologists such as Warren K. Bickel and Marc N. Potenza recognize that addiction "emerges from the interaction of evolutionarily old behavioral processes and their associated brain regions. . . . Many of these subunits developed and were passed on by natural selection because they conveyed survival advantages" (Bickel and Potenza 2006, 9). Chemicals involved in neuro-transmission reward useful behaviors such as eating and sex; thus, "pleasure has an evolutionary purpose" (Sheff 2013, 9). The American Society of Addiction Medicine concludes:

> Addiction is a primary, chronic disease of brain reward, motivation, memory and related circuitry. Dysfunction in these circuits leads to characteristic biological, psychological, social and spiritual manifestations. This is reflected in an individual pathologically pursuing reward and/or relief by substance use and other behaviors. (American Society of Addiction Medicine 2014, accessed September 2014)

It is a bitter irony that the peril of addiction is based upon survival mechanisms inherent in the process of evolution.

Characteristics of Addiction

With subtle variations, contemporary writers are in agreement on the nature of addiction. Bickel and Potenza posit four characteristics: (1) "frequent ingestion or engagement," (2) "emergent behavior," (3) "negative life consequences," and (4) "additional energy must be added to the system to alter an otherwise stable system" (Bickel and Potenza 2006, 15–16). George F. Koob specifies that addiction is "a chronically relapsing disorder characterized by (1) a compulsion to seek and take the drug, (2) loss of control in limiting intake, and (3) emergence of a negative emotional state . . . when access to the drug is prevented" (Koob 2006, 25). Gerald May lists five properties of addiction: "(1) tolerance, (2) withdrawal, (3) self-deception, (4) loss of willpower, and (5) distortion of attention" (May 1991, 26). Finally, the ASAM identifies five "behavioral manifestations and complications" of addiction (see Appendix A), while the DSM-5 provides a list of eleven characteristics of substance addiction such as alcoholism (see Appendix B) and nine characteristics of non-substance related disorders such as gambling (see Appendix C). Characteristics on which there is general agreement include erosion of control and loss of willpower, compulsive behavior, development of tolerance, and the phenomena of withdrawal.

Neurobiology of Addiction

The review of contemporary literature would not be complete without acknowledging current discussion on the status of addiction theory which emphasizes the impact of addiction on the brain, specifically the role of addictive substances in neurotransmission. Here there is marked consensus among addictionologists. Anna Rose Childress reports that the function of neurotransmitters has gained recognition in the study of addiction, particularly dopamine's effect on the nucleus accumbens. As she notes, "*dopamine* has been the focus of most research attention in human brain-imaging studies" (Childress 2006, 50; italics hers). Harvard Medical School confirms this view: "In the brain, pleasure has a distinct signature: the release of the neurotransmitter dopamine in the nucleus accumbens" (Harvard Medical School 2011, 1). Whether a substance or behavior will lead to addiction is "directly linked to the speed with which it promotes dopamine release, the intensity of that release, and the reliability of that release" (Harvard Medical School 2011, 2). Addictive drugs can release two to ten times the amount of dopamine that normal activities do. Over time, however, the brain may adapt to the increased levels of dopamine, a phenomena known as tolerance.

Ultimately, "dopamine interacts with another neurotransmitter, glutamate, to take over the brain's system of reward-related learning" (Harvard Medical School 2011, 2). The ASAM concludes, "At the neurotransmitter level, addiction-related adaptations have been documented not only for dopamine but also for glutamate" (Volkow and Warren 2014, 7). Therefore, in addition to pleasure, addiction relies on learning and memory, which center in the hippocampus and amygdala, and result in the phenomena of craving. Daniel Lende remarks, "'dopamine and glutamate make up the disease of addiction'. . . . Addiction is not just pleasure and craving. It is also about learning and memory" (Lende 2010, accessed January 2016). T. M. Tzschentke and W. J. Schmidt emphasize the importance of glutamate in learning:

> Traditionally, addiction research in neuroscience has focused on mechanisms involving dopamine and endogenous opioids. More recently, it has been realized that glutamate also plays a central role in processes underlying the development and maintenance of addiction. These processes include reinforcement, sensitization, habit learning and reinforcement learning, context conditioning, craving and relapse. (Tzschentke and Schmidt 2003, 373)

Sheff sums it up, "a hallmark of the disease of addiction is the altered flow of neurotransmitters, especially dopamine. . . . The brain is hijacked" (Sheff 2013, 91–92). Study of the neurobiology of addiction is based not only on theory, but also on the science of brain-imaging and observation of brain scans, and thereby warrants reference in the syllabus.

Addiction as a Syndrome or Spectrum Disorder

Today there is marked agreement among scientists that addiction is a syndrome or spectrum disorder, as White suggests:

> It wasn't until the 2000s that addiction was fully articulated as a spectrum disorder. . . . 1) discovery of common neurobiological roots (reward pathways) for what had previously been viewed as quite distinct substance use disorders, 2) discovery that these common reward pathways are also shared by various "process addictions," e.g. gambling, and 3) studies suggesting that genetic vulnerability for

addiction was not substance-specific. These suggested a "common underlying addiction process." (White 2014, 436)

Howard J. Shaffer concurs in his article, "Toward A Syndrome Model of Addiction: Multiple Expressions, Common Etiology" (Shaffer et al. 2004, 367–74), that "addiction should be understood as a syndrome with multiple opportunistic expressions" (Shaffer et al. 2004, 367). Shaffer has led the way in observing that "addictive disorders might not be independent" of each other, that there are shared "neurobiological antecedents," "shared psychosocial antecedents" and "shared experiences" (Shaffer et al. 2004, 367). He references studies showing that many people are "dependent on multiple substances, raising the possibility of a general addictive tendency" (Shaffer et al. 2004, 369). Different drugs and behaviors stimulate the brain's dopamine reward system in much the same way. "Psychosocial factors supplement the underlying neurobiological risk" in a way that is not substance-or-behavior specific (Shaffer et al. 2004, 369). The same "neurobiological circuitry of the central nervous system is the ultimate common pathway for addictive behaviors" (Shaffer et al. 2004, 369). Neuroadaptations such as developing tolerance and experiencing withdrawal are similar for different addictions. Finally, "Scientific evidence suggests that behaviors, such as excessive gambling, and substance use, such as cocaine, have similar effects on the neurocircuitry of reward" (Shaffer 2012, accessed January 2016). Therefore, Shaffer proposes that, "the neurobiological and psychosocial antecedent evidence for the syndrome model is strong" (Shaffer et al. 2004, 372). Shaffer is widely respected as a proponent of the syndrome model of addiction. Addictions were formerly considered as "co-occurring" or examples of "co-morbidity," but due to Shaffer and others today they are viewed as aspects of a spectrum disorder, much as autism has been regarded for some time. A syllabus for pastors must embrace this concept.[4]

---

4. It should be noted that in addition to potential drug and alcohol abuse, Christian leaders and pastors themselves are particularly vulnerable to food, workaholism, and sex addiction. Bob Burns, Tasha D. Chapman and Donald C. Guthrie explain, "one study shows that 76 percent of clergy were either overweight or obese, compared to 61 percent of the general population" (Burns, Chapman and Guthrie 2013, 61). Furthermore, workaholism is cited from the writing of Bryan Robinson as an example of "an obsessive-compulsive disorder that manifests itself through . . . an overindulgence in work" (Burns, Chapman, and Guthrie 2013, 76). Finally, Patrick A. Means reports, "Surveys show that 50 to 60 percent of Christian men have a problem with porn. Many believe the number is higher" (Means 2006, 9). Means proceeds to report the results of a survey of Christian leaders including pastors: "64 percent struggle with sexual addiction or sexual compulsion, including but not limited to the use of pornography" (Means 2006, 132–33). The

Issues from Related Contemporary Literature
Workshop Training and Leadership

The deep background of this writer's workshop training and performance on the subject supplements his review of contemporary literature on addiction theory. This writer attended a Mariner's Hospital lecture series on this topic by Dr. Eugene L. Manuel in Tavernier, Florida on January 29, 2013. It was from Dr. Manuel that he first heard basic concepts about addiction, specifically the neurochemical changes in the brain by addictive substances.

This researcher then participated in the "Fifth Annual Mental and Behavioral Health Symposium" at Baptist Hospital in Miami on March 2, 2013. Major presenters were Michael J. Herkov on "The Addictions," Ingrid Barrera on "Food Addiction: Eating Disorders and Obesity," and Elizabeth A. Crocco speaking on "Prescription Drug Abuse in the Elderly." Dr. John C. Eustace, medical director of the South Miami Hospital Addiction Treatment and Recovery Center, was the chief speaker on the "Neurobiology of Addictions: From Adolescence Through Adulthood," emphasizing that 15 percent of our population is addicted.

Eustace presented a comprehensive view of addiction medicine, such as biogenetics, the dopamine reward system, and neuroimaging studies including PET (Positron Emission Tomography) and SPECT (Single-Photon Emission Computerized Tomography) scans, and areas and functions of the brain, notably the nucleus accumbens. He discussed types of addiction including process addictions with an emphasis on sex addiction, co-occurring disorders, and pharmacologic and non-pharmacologic interventions. This writer had formerly seen addiction only in the context of the Twelve Step movement. Eustace and others now opened a brave, new world—the science of addiction.

On February 19, 2014, this researcher participated in another workshop at the Baptist Hospital in Miami led by Dr. John C. Eustace and David Vittoria on "Dealing with Transference and Counter-Transference in the Care of the Addicted Patient." On September 19, 2014, this writer attended when this seminar was given a second time to a different audience at Mariner's Hospital, in Tavernier, Florida. Vittoria is the Assistant Vice President of the South Miami Hospital Addiction Treatment and Recovery Center. In treatment for addiction, Vittoria emphasized the phenomena of transference, which occurs between an addict and his helper—it is the unconscious tendency to assign to others in one's present life feelings and attitudes

---

subject of addiction among clergy warrants a study of its own.

associated with significant others early in life. In short, the client transfers emotions from the past onto present players in his life. Countertransference is the response of the caregiver to the client's unconscious transference. Instead of merely reacting, what is needed are appropriate and emphatic responses from the caregiver. As in earlier workshops, Eustace emphasized areas and function of the brain involved in addiction, including the use of SPECT and PET scans, and acknowledged how substance use problems are part of a syndrome or spectrum disorder. In managing transference, Eustace stressed the reality that it will occur, and the importance of objectivity, clarity, and honesty.

Finally, on February 28, 2015, this writer presented one of the major talks in a symposium at Baptist Hospital in Miami on "Resilience in Addiction Recovery." In this presentation, he referred to resilience in his own experiences, spoke of the limited resilience of churches, commended the field of addiction theory for its insight and resilience, despaired of the backward resilience of American society, and acknowledged the mixed resilience of the addiction treatment industry. (For a copy of the PowerPoint slides for this presentation, see Figure 2.)

Issues from Related Contemporary Literature

RESILIENCE IN ADDICTION RECOVERY Herbert E. Hudson IV	**RESILIENCE OF CHURCHES** • Role of Churches in Temperance and Prohibition (1920–1932) • A.A. founded in 1935 • View of Churches Toward A.A./Twelve Step Recovery
RESILIENCE OF MEDICAL AND TREATMENT PARADIGMS Spectrum Disorder (example: Autism), and Syndrome Model (example: AIDS)—Howard Shaffer • Common neurobiological reward pathways of AOD's (Alcohol and Other Drugs) • Shared by Process Addictions • Common underlying addiction process	**RESILENCE OF SOCIETY** • 1930s–1980s Disease stemming from biopsychosocial vulnerability • Since 1980, addiction coming to be viewed more as willful and criminal behavior • De-medicalization and more emphasis on criminalization. • 2.4 million now incarcerated, 4 times the number of 1980, 85% because of crimes related to drugs
RESILIENCE NEEDED IN TREATMENT ATTITUDES • John Mendelson • William L. White • Harold Hughes	**A FINAL NOTE ON RESILIENCE** • Recovery is my most sacred possession, and it's complex and confusing and uncomfortable and emotionally messy—and yes, it is worth it! (Paraphrased from William L. White) • Of Men and Star Fish

Figure 2.
PowerPoint slides for "Resilience in Addiction Recovery Symposium," February 28, 2015.

LITERATURE ON THE GENERAL SUBJECT OF ADDICTION TREATMENT

In the development of a syllabus for clergy, the final issue is addiction treatment, which has also received widespread attention among contemporary writers. Major contributors to the discussion of addiction treatment are Room, Mann, Jellinek, White, Miller, and Rollnick.

Robin Room

One of the lesser known but most prolific writers in the field of alcoholism is sociologist Robin Room—he has edited and written thirty books and nearly three hundred journal articles. In conjunction with Don Cahalan, he contributed to the major sociological report on alcoholism in America, *Problem Drinking Among American Men* (Cahalan and Room 1974). Under the sponsorship of the National Institute of Mental Health this study reported findings of two national surveys and an in-depth study in San Francisco. In this comprehensive work, Room and Cahalan set the tone for future studies of alcoholism as a public health issue. From the viewpoint of a social scientist, Room gives an insightful and useful perspective of "Alcoholics Anonymous as a Social Movement" in a chapter in *Research on Alcoholics Anonymous: Opportunities and Alternatives* (Room 1993, 163–87). He discusses the extent of membership in Twelve Step groups, organizational principles of A.A. (referring to how much of A.A. is carried on in an oral, as opposed to a written, tradition), and the future of A.A., including whether it will "eventually reach a saturation point... [and deplete] the population pool from which [it draws]" (Room 1993, 185). During the last half of the twentieth century, Room may well have been the most inexhaustible writer in the field of alcoholism and addiction. The perspective of social sciences is clearly appropriate for inclusion in a course for clergy.

Marty Mann

Marty Mann was one of the first women to get sober through Alcoholics Anonymous, and in 1944 she was the founder of the National Committee for Education on Alcoholism. Other early women in A.A. included Lil and Sylvia K. from Akron, and Florence Rankin in New York; the latter authored the story in the first edition of *Alcoholics Anonymous* titled, "A Feminine

Victory." Mann spent her life shaping national policy toward alcoholism and mobilizing treatment and educational resources. She was not only active in A.A., but helped found the Yale Center of Alcohol Studies and the Research Council on Problems of Alcohol. Her book, *New Primer on Alcoholism: How People Drink, How to Recognize Alcoholics, and What to do About Them* (Mann 1950), pioneered the study of alcoholism as a public health issue. She considered alcoholism as a disease, and the alcoholic as a sick person who can be helped and who is worth helping. Her book states: "Alcoholism is a disease which manifests itself chiefly by the uncontrollable drinking of the victim, who is known as an alcoholic. It is a progressive... and often a fatal, disease... *if* it is not treated and arrested. But it can be arrested" (Mann 1981, 3; italics hers). With the exception of Linda Mercadante, we have had few opportunities to hear a feminist perspective—Wilson even rebuffed the request of his wife, Lois, to write part of the *Big Book*. Marty Mann has a voice that needs to be heard in this discussion.

E. Morton Jellinek

Mann's scientific collaborator was Yale scientist E. Morton Jellinek who published his study, *The Disease Concept of Alcoholism* (Jellinek 1960), which established the precedent in treatment for considering addiction as an illness and furthered the medicalization of alcoholism. Jellinek deals with the loss of control, early stages of tolerance and habituation, concepts of craving and compulsion, psychological aspects, psychopathological and other physical formulations, alcoholism as an allergy, and alcoholism as a form of "brain pathology" (Jellinek 1960, 88–91). Jellinek also acknowledges, "One of the greatest roles in bringing the illness conception to the widest reaches of public opinion was played by the fellowship of Alcoholics Anonymous" (Jellinek 1960, 10). As previously noted, authors who disagreed with Jellinek on the disease concept of alcoholism included Herbert Fingarette, whose book *Heavy Drinking: The Myth of Alcoholism as a Disease* (Fingarette 1988) is a definitive statement of that position. Jellinek provided an indispensable link between early alcohol treatment and that which followed. His pivotal work needs to be recognized in a syllabus for ministers.

William L. White

Years later, William L. White made an invaluable and exhaustive survey of addiction treatment in the United States in his book *Slaying the Dragon: The History of Addiction Treatment and Recovery in America* (White 2014). In addition, White co-authored eighteen other books and over four hundred articles on the subject. He occupies a unique place as a writer on the history of addiction treatment, and his work has become a benchmark by which other books on the history of treatment are measured. For example, he chronicles the contributions of Bill Wilson's physician, William Duncan Silkworth, who treated over fifty thousand alcoholics at the Charles B. Towns Hospital and Knickerbocker Hospital in New York. "Silkworth's suggestion of a constitutional vulnerability which prompted alcoholics to drink—out of necessity rather than choice—became the cornerstone of the modern disease concept of alcoholism" (White 2014, 187). White proceeds to critique the role of addiction treatment: "Contempt, often mutual, is an enduring and troubling theme in the historical relationship between helping professionals and people experiencing addiction" (White 2014, 515). As he observes, "There is no other major health problem for which one is admitted for professional care and then punitively discharged from treatment for becoming symptomatic in the service setting" (White 2014, 519).

White documents the role of Senator Harold Hughes, who was a three-term governor of Iowa and a member of Alcoholics Anonymous. Hughes was one of the first to indict current alcoholism treatment: "[Hughes] often noted that alcoholism was the only disorder in which the patient was blamed when treatment failed" (White 2014, 513). Hughes was responsible for introducing the "Comprehensive Alcohol Abuse and Alcoholism Prevention, Treatment, and Rehabilitation Act" in 1970, better known as the "Hughes Act," which opened the door for treatment of alcohol and drug addiction. Kurtz commented that it "would profoundly change everything concerning alcoholism and its treatment in the culture of the United States" (Kurtz 2002, 33, accessed July 2015).

William R. Miller and Stephen Rollnick

In 1991, William R. Miller and Stephen Rollnick contributed to the dialogue on addiction treatment with their book *Motivational Interviewing: Helping People Change*, now in its third edition. It occupies a singular place

Issues from Related Contemporary Literature

in the current discussion of addiction treatment. Motivational Interviewing (MI) is an authoritative approach to facilitating change in those who are troubled, including alcoholics and addicts. As the authors state, "MI has taken root in caring for some of the most neglected and rejected members of society" (Miller and Rollnick 2013, 381). Techniques that do not work with addicts are confrontation and punishment; what does work are feedback, encouragement, empathy, and support for self-efficacy. The book elucidates the four processes of Motivational Interviewing—engaging, focusing, evoking, and planning—and illustrates what they look like in practice (Miller and Rollnick 2013, 25–30). Basic skills include asking open questions, affirming, reflective listening, and summarizing (Miller and Rollnick 2013, 33–35). Numerous interview examples and stories illustrate the "do's and don'ts" of implementation in different settings. The importance of Miller and Rollnick's study cannot be overestimated. It has served as a text and guide for countless therapists inside and outside of the field of addiction recovery, and would be an excellent resource for the counseling role of clergy.

SUMMARY

In this chapter, this writer has traced the ongoing discussion among various authors and has reviewed contemporary literature that relates to six issues. This presents a comprehensive survey of addiction, history, and concepts on which to base a syllabus that may address the following:

1. Knowledge deficits in the area of addictionology: Although most clergy and seminary presidents believe addiction is a serious problem, only small percentages receive or offer training on the subject.

2. History and background of Twelve Step programs: The Emmanuel Movement and the Oxford Group contributed to the forming of Alcoholics Anonymous, and A.A. itself can be understood as the progeny of its co-founders, Bill Wilson and Dr. Bob Smith.

3. Explanation of how Twelve Step organizations work: Both Alcoholics Anonymous and Christ-centered programs such as Celebrate Recovery embody Twelve Step principles; their canonical documents disclose how they function.

4. Spiritual features of the Twelve Step design and its relationship to Christianity: Admission of personal powerlessness and reliance upon the grace of God of their understanding are fundamental to overcoming unhealthy attachments.

5. Current information on addiction theory: Addiction is a product of an evolutionary survival mechanism, has predictable and consistent characteristics, involves addictive substances in neurotransmission resulting in the brain being hijacked, and is a syndrome or spectrum disorder.

6. The general subject of addiction treatment: Addiction is an illness or disease treatable by the medical profession and qualified counselors, which requires that judgment and contempt be set aside in favor of empathy and self-efficacy.

Chapter 4

Narrative of Research Execution

A NARRATIVE OF THE research in this study includes methodology, execution, replication of the study, and a general observation on the pastorate.

METHODOLOGY

The purpose of the field research was to inform the writing of a syllabus for those in ministerial training. The data was collected from pastors in an area particularly devastated by addiction, the Florida Keys,[1] and who were active in either the Upper Keys Ministerial Association or the Key West Ministerial Alliance. The most efficient way of obtaining information was deemed to be through written surveys and face-to-face interviews. Personal observation, case studies, and focus groups were considered, but judged to be less effective in securing the needed data.

As a retired minister, this researcher was active as a member of the clergy community in the Florida Keys and had engaged in personal communication with other pastors on this subject for many years. He was able to use the knowledge gained from these interactions to inform the creation of a survey that produced discrete and measurable data for this study. The written survey is what is known as a "single-stage sampling," or a cross-sectional design "with the data collected at one point in time" (Creswell 2014, 158, 157). John W. Creswell asserts that the purpose of a survey is "to generalize from a sample to a population so that inferences can be made about some characteristic, attitude, or behavior of this population"

---

1. See the study previously cited from the University of Washington, showing that residents of the Florida Keys drink "at higher rates than . . . Miami neighbors, or any other Florida county" (Gore 2015, accessed February 2016).

(Creswell 2014, 157). Structured interviews were added to gain deeper knowledge of a representative sample of respondents. Since the written survey was mainly quantitative and the interviews were primarily qualitative, the result was a mixed-methods approach that allowed quantifiable study and in-depth exploration of particular topics.

As mentioned, subjects were drawn from the Upper Keys Ministerial Association and the Key West Ministerial Alliance, the two major ministerial groups in Monroe County, Florida. This writer was an active member of the Upper Keys Ministerial Association, and had a working relationship with its executive officer. Furthermore, he had been to meetings of the Key West Ministerial Alliance and had known one of its leading members for many years from Upstate New York. Thus, he had a personal connection with gatekeepers and ready access to the sample groups. Because he was known to some of the subjects, this researcher had to be especially careful not to disclose bias in the conduct of this study.

Since the subjects were not randomly selected, they were a "nonprobability sample (or *convenience sample)*, in which respondents were chosen based on their convenience and availability" (Creswell 2014, 158; italics his). The research, then, fell into the category of a "quasi-experiment" (Creswell 2014, 168). The result was a pilot study, which can be replicated in other communities. Outcomes in other locations, however, may vary somewhat due to the relatively unique cultural setting of the current study and its limitations in sample size and selection.

The survey instrument used to collect data was a mixed-methods questionnaire designed by this writer (for a copy of the questionnaire, see Appendix D). An Informed Consent statement was included in the survey. Human Rights in Research protocol was observed in all phases of this research. A preliminary draft of survey and interview questions was closely scrutinized, and resulted in the elimination of some questions and the rewording of others.

The survey employed primarily closed questions (quantitative) that utilized a Likert five point agree/disagree scale with a middle option. In addition to establishing basic demographic data, self-rated responses were utilized to ascertain familiarity with and attitude toward addiction and the Twelve Step approach. Primary administration of the survey was at regularly scheduled meetings of each ministerial group, taking fifteen to twenty minutes of their program time. After a short introduction, which included discussion of Human Rights issues, participants had approximately fifteen minutes to complete the printed forms. They had not seen the questions ahead of time, and this researcher remained in the room to answer questions. The group leader then collected and delivered completed surveys to this writer. Secondary administration of the survey was done individually with some of those not at ministerial meetings.

The second part of the research methodology was qualitative interviews. These also were from a nonrandom sample, in which pastors who took the written survey self-selected to participate further—a type of "snowball effect" (for a copy of the interview questions, see Appendix F). Interviews were semi-structured, with "specific questions that are organized by topics but are not necessarily asked in a specified order," which at times reverted to dialogue (Bailey 2007, 100). The interviews occurred in a confidential setting, such as the subject's office, and this researcher attempted to maintain a neutral attitude. Prior to the interviews, participants read and signed an "Informed Consent Statement" (a copy is attached as Appendix E). Observation protocol for the interview included manual note-taking and utilization of a digital voice recorder. During every stage of the methodology implementation, this writer recorded gathered data. This researcher then evaluated completed surveys, interview recordings, and observation notes. They were stored in this writer's office; he destroyed interview recordings after the work was completed.

RESEARCH EXECUTION

This researcher conducted the surveys and interviews in the Florida Keys during April 2016. No compensation was offered for participation, but this researcher indicated he would share results with those who were interested. He deliberately chose the period following Lent and Easter when he thought pastors would be most available. There were approximately sixty-four active clergy in the Keys, as reported by leaders of the ministerial groups. This study surveyed 27–42 percent of the total, and interviewed 14–22 percent of the total.

This researcher administered surveys at the Upper Keys Ministerial Association meeting on April 7, 2016. Advance sign-up was not required to participate in the survey. Attendance at this meeting was below average and only five surveys were completed. He then surveyed members of the Key West Ministerial Alliance on April 12, but again attendance was relatively low and produced only seven results. Partly as the result of low attendance at ministerial meetings, the researcher gained access to and was given permission to use lists of active ministers in each of the groups. In addition to Catholic and traditional Protestant denominations, lists included clergy of Unitarian, Unity, and Jewish congregations. During the remainder of April, he randomly conducted an additional fifteen individual surveys. One pastor who was ill requested a survey by telephone; the results were similar to surveys done face to face. Typically, surveys took fifteen to twenty minutes to complete.

This researcher conducted all the interviews in person, meeting in a confidential location such as the office of the interviewee. After general conversation, the researcher asked the interviewee to read and sign the Informed Consent Statement, and asked for permission to audio-record the interview. Only one clergyperson who was interviewed declined being audio-recorded. In addition to the audio recording, the interviewer took notes on his observations of the interview. Within a few hours after the interview, he transcribed the recordings into written form. The interviewer followed the sequence of the planned questions, and he was careful not to express an opinion on them. More than once ministers remarked, "I can't tell what you are thinking" (Interview by author, Florida Keys, April 6, 2016), which lent credence to the effectiveness of the interviewer's impartiality. Interviews took thirty to forty minutes to complete.

REPLICATING THE RESEARCH

The field research is eminently reproducible in other locations, in order to broaden existing data in support of education for those in ministerial training, or to design a response of the clergy's role in addiction recovery in a particular community. In replicating the survey, the following suggestions are offered:

1. From the experience of having conducted the surveys and interviews this writer would recommend the addition of the following survey questions with response options of (1) Strongly Agree, (2) Somewhat Agree, (3) Neutral, (4) Somewhat Disagree, (5) Strongly Disagree:

    A. "Do you preach a sermon on addiction recovery at least once a year?"

    B. "When you were in seminary, were courses offered in addiction recovery?"

Narrative of Research Execution

   C. "While in seminary, did you take a course in addiction recovery?"

   D. "Is addiction both a sin and a disease?"

2. Throughout the research, Human Rights in Research should be closely observed.

3. The first decision is to decide how to conduct the surveys. As in the case of the current study, surveys could be done in person. In other situations where this is impractical, surveys can be done by mail or electronically.

4. A critical step is to compile a master list of all clergy names, denominations, and contact information. This list should be provided by a reputable source, such as a local Council of Churches or Ministerial Association, and permission should be obtained for its use.

5. Whether the surveys are in person or by mail, the most important thing is having them returned. This may require persistent follow-up. This is one of the advantages of giving the surveys in person.

6. After they are returned, responses to each question should be recorded on a master list, such as a spreadsheet program. Likert scale answers may be assigned the following values: Strongly Agree (1), Somewhat Agree (2), Neutral or No Opinion (3), Somewhat Disagree (4), and Strongly Disagree (5). The spreadsheet can then be programed to give averages, standard deviations, and even coefficients of correlation, if desired, to facilitate evaluation and reporting.

7. Pastors will naturally be curious about the results. Follow-up, including a thank you, is a common courtesy.

The following suggestions are offered in replicating the interviews:

1. Interview subjects may have already taken the survey, so the interview provides an opportunity for in-depth exploration.

2. The interviewer may be the individual who administered the survey, but in situations where there are many subjects, this may not be practical and additional interviewers may need to be recruited. In this event, their training becomes critical.

3. Interviews are scheduled in a one-on-one setting where the subject is comfortable and secure. Typically, this is in the interviewee's office or residence, which requires additional time spent in travel by the interviewer.

4. It is recommended that interviews be done in person, rather than by telephone.

5. It is important to allow five to ten minutes for preliminaries before beginning the interview proper. Interviews can be completed in thirty minutes, and should probably not exceed an hour.

6. In addition to the interviewer taking notes, a recording device is essential to ensure accuracy of direct quotations. The recordings should be transcribed into written form at the earliest opportunity. It is courteous to ask permission before the recorder is turned on, and it is prudent to destroy recordings when the study is completed.

7. Again, a follow-up and thank-you are in order.

OBSERVATION ON THE PASTORATE AND SUMMARY

Interviews offered an occasion for this researcher to meet and become better acquainted with other local pastors. The time before the actual interview included fellowship, general conversation, and sometimes prayer. With only a few exceptions, pastors seemed eager to have a colleague to share with and confide in from outside their church. Sometimes they talked about personal matters in their lives or work. They seemed hungry for discussion with a peer and appreciated the time together. This writer was reminded of the axiom: "The pastorate is sometimes a lonely profession."

In this chapter the researcher has discussed methodology, research execution, possible replication of the study, and an observation on the pastorate.

Chapter 5

Research Evaluation

THIS RESEARCHER GROUPED AND analyzed both quantitative data from the surveys and qualitative responses from the interviews according to the initial goals of this study, to determine "whether the hypotheses or questions were supported or whether they were refuted" (Creswell 2014, 178). In considering each of the goals, this report determined the variation of scores, and triangulated responses for patterns, generalizations, and correlations. A general narrative of what pastors shared is included in this evaluation summary.

FIRST GOAL: UNDERSTANDING PRE-CONDITIONS OF PASTORS' VIEWS

The first goal of this study is to understand the pre-conditions that might influence the views of pastors toward the Twelve Step paradigm. The objectives of this goal are the following: to ascertain the role of family history and personal experience among clergy; to consider the influence of age and gender of pastors; to determine the impact of denominational affiliation; and to reflect on the effect of seminary training and other education, notably in social sciences.

Family History and Personal Experience with Addiction

Table 1. History of Addiction in Families of Pastors

	Yes	No	No Answer
Question 24: History of Addiction in Your Family?	89 percent (24)	11 percent (3)	0 (0)

Note: Figures in parentheses are base numbers for the adjacent percentages.

The findings in Table 1 were striking. Eighty-nine percent of pastors surveyed experienced addiction in their families; only 11 percent did not. In other words, almost 90 percent of pastors reported having a family member who suffered from addiction. Nine out of ten clergy having family members with addiction problems is an impressive ratio. In order to protect Human Rights in Research, there were no questions asking whether pastors had a personal history of addiction.

Family history and the personal impact of addiction was a theme often repeated in interviews. A pastor related about growing up in the inner city: "I probably buried almost half of my friends because of addiction or what they got involved in because of addiction" (Interview by author, Florida Keys, April 4).[1] One pastor confided about an alcoholic parent being physically abusive. Another pastor disclosed in an interview:

> I've seen alcohol addiction destroy my own family. My biological mother was alcoholic, gave me up for adoption at birth because of her alcoholism. I know she would have cut her arm off to beat her alcohol condition, but couldn't. And eventually she lost her life. My brother and his wife both died from alcohol abuse. (Interview by author, Florida Keys, April 14)

---

1. All interviews were confidential; the names of interviewees are withheld by mutual agreement. Names of specific towns in the Florida Keys are also withheld to protect anonymity of participants.

Research Evaluation

Age and Gender

Table 2. Age of Pastors

	18–25	26–30	31–40	41–50	51–60	61+
Question 19: Age?	0	0	15 percent (4)	15 percent (4)	26 percent (7)	44 percent (12)

	Yes	No				
Question 21: Now Work as Minister?	96 percent (26)	4 percent (1)				

Note: Figures in parentheses are base numbers for the adjacent percentages.

As seen in Table 2, 44 percent of pastors surveyed were of retirement age (sixty-one and older), 70 percent of pastors polled were fifty-one and older, only 30 percent were fifty and younger. (For a graph of age distribution of clergy, see Figure 3 below.) Almost half of pastors surveyed in the Keys were of retirement age, and nearly three-quarters were over fifty. Ninety-six percent currently worked in ministry, while 4 percent did not. It appears that many pastors who are of retirement age preferred to stay active in ministry in Monroe County.

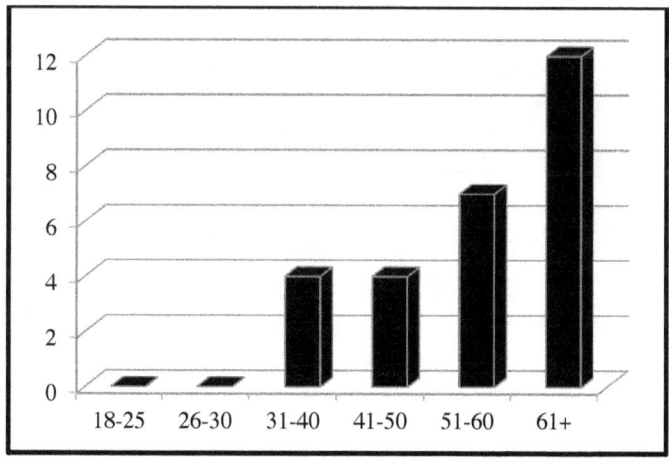

Figure 3. Age of Pastors. Source: Survey, 2016.

Table 3. Gender of Pastors

	Male	Female
Question 20: Gender?	74 percent (20)	26 percent (7)

Note: Figures in parentheses are base numbers for the adjacent percentages.

The gender distribution of pastors who were surveyed, as reflected in Table 3, was disproportionately high for females. In 2010, the Faith Communities Today survey of eleven thousand American congregations "found 12 percent of all U.S. congregations had a woman senior or sole ordained leader" (Women Clergy 2015, accessed September 2016). Over twice that number, or 26 percent of clergy in the Florida Keys who were polled, were female. In other words, there were twice as many women ministers in the Florida Keys as compared to other parts of the country. There was no noticeable correlation between age or gender and pastors' views toward addiction recovery and Twelve Step programs.

Denominational Affiliation

Table 4. Denomination of pastors

Question 1: Denominational affiliation?	
Baptist	7 percent (2)
Methodist	11 percent (3)
Church of Christ	4 percent (1)
Lutheran	7 percent (2)
Episcopal	7 percent (2)
Presbyterian	4 percent (1)
Unitarian	4 percent (1)
Catholic	11 percent (3)
Other	44 percent (12)

Note: Figures in parentheses are base numbers for the adjacent percentages.

Research Evaluation

Table 4 presents the distribution of pastors by denomination. In general, there did not seem to be significant correlations between denominational affiliation and views toward Twelve Step organizations. Three pastors who were not from "mainline" Protestant denominations, however, gave responses that were noticeably more negative toward addiction and Twelve Step programs.[2] Designated as Pastors A, B, and C, their answers to several questions fell significantly above the mean, as shown in Table 5 below. In tabulating results, scores from Likert scale answers were assigned as follows: Strongly Agree (1), Somewhat Agree (2), Neutral or No Opinion (3), Somewhat Disagree (4), and Strongly Disagree (5).

Table 5. Responses of Pastors Not from Mainline Protestant Churches

	Mean	Pastor A	Pastor B	Pastor C
Question 11: Addiction a Disease, Not Sin?	2.48	4	4	4
Question 13: Favorable to Twelve Step Groups?	1.19	2	2	3
Question 14: Twelve Steps Based on Christianity?	2.22	4	2	4

Educational Background

Table 6. Education of Pastors

	Yes	No	No Answer
Question 22: Graduate from Seminary?	74 percent (20)	26 percent (7)	0
Question 23: Further Post-Graduate Education in Social Sciences?	44 percent (12)	56 percent (15)	0

Note: Figures in parentheses are base numbers for the adjacent percentages.

---

2. "Mainline" churches generally refer to American Baptist, United Methodist, United Church of Christ, Evangelical Lutheran, Episcopal, Presbyterian, and Disciples of Christ. The classification of not "mainline" is intended as descriptive, not judgmental.

Seventy-four percent of clergy reported graduating from seminary and 26 percent had no formal ministerial training, as is indicated in Table 6. Forty-four percent of the pastors reported receiving post-graduate education in social sciences and 56 percent did not. Put another way, over one-quarter of the pastors did not have the benefit of a seminary education. On the other hand, almost half of the clergy surveyed had completed graduate work in some branch of the social sciences. A few pastors who were interviewed related that they had advanced ministerial degrees—three had doctorates. Several had degrees and certifications in social work. One clergyperson's primary occupation was as a child-welfare social worker dealing with domestic violence and substance abuse. That minister believed that almost all of his clients struggled with addiction. Except for this pastor, there did not appear to be a correlation between educational background and attitudes toward addiction recovery. None of those interviewed were required to take a course on addiction in their seminary, and none could remember if such a course was offered, unless perhaps as a part of a concentration in pastoral counseling.

SECOND GOAL: ASCERTAINING HOW INFORMED PASTORS ARE ON ADDICTION AND THE TWELVE STEP FORMAT

The second goal was to ascertain how informed pastors are about addiction and the Twelve Step format. The objectives of this goal were as follows: to establish knowledgeability of pastors on the problem of addiction in general; to determine how familiar pastors are with the Twelve Step philosophy; to explore how aware clergy are of Christ-based Twelve Step programs; and to ascertain the perception of pastors about parishioners who have addictions.

RESEARCH EVALUATION

Knowledgeability on Addiction in General

Table 7. How Knowledgeable Pastors Are on Addiction

	Strongly Agree	Somewhat Agree	Neutral/ No Opinion	Somewhat Disagree	Strongly Disagree	No Answer
Question 9: Familiar with Addiction and Recovery?	78 percent (21)	19 percent (5)	4 percent (1)	0	0	0
Question 10: Is Addiction Significant Problem?	70 percent (19)	30 percent (8)	0	0	0	0

Note: Figures in parentheses are base numbers for the adjacent percentages.

Despite the moderate level of formal training in addiction, including that gained in social sciences, pastors reported a high degree of familiarity with addiction. When asked if they were familiar with addiction recovery, as referred to in Table 7, 78 percent of clergy strongly agreed and 19 percent somewhat agreed. As mentioned previously, pastors reported in interviews that what they have learned about addiction has not been from formal course work, but through self-study and practical experience. More than once pastors commented that they learned about addiction from a spouse who was a professional. One learned from a partner who is a counselor and did a supervised internship in an addiction clinic. Table 7 also reveals that 70 percent of pastors strongly agreed and 30 percent somewhat agreed that addiction is a significant problem. This was an impressively high level of agreement that addiction is a major concern today. There was little deviation in answers, and no one disputed that addiction is a critical issue.

Table 8. Florida Keys Susceptible to Addiction

	Yes	No	Don't Know	No Answer
Question 2: Keys More Susceptible to Addictive Life Style?	82 percent (22)	7 percent (2)	11 percent (3)	0

Note: Figures in parentheses are base numbers for the adjacent percentages.

Table 8 shows that 82 percent of clergy agreed that the Florida Keys are more susceptible to an addictive life style than many other parts of the country. In interviews, pastors frequently referred to the seriousness of addiction in Monroe County. One clergyperson exclaimed, "Horrendous, huge, it's immense. . . . There's probably more addiction in the Keys than there is in all of Miami-Dade. I personally know of two people who committed suicide . . . because of addiction" (Interview by author, Florida Keys, April 4). A minister who does a great deal of counseling reflected in an interview that addiction in the Keys is massive, "five times the national average" (Interview by author, Florida Keys, April 8). Another member of the clergy insisted, "This place has more visible addiction than any place I've ever lived" (Interview by author, Florida Keys, April 26). This researcher was impressed by how clearly and strongly clergy expressed themselves on the subject. One pastor offered this graphic assessment:

> I would say that in the community at large, it's the #1 issue. . . . To be probably less tactful than I could be, the Florida Keys act like the P-trap of the United States. You know, under your sink you have the P-trap. . . . I think people because of climate, end up funneling South. I think people who want to drop out and slide away, end up here. We know we are one of the top counties in the nation, I think it's #2 for disease, the number of divorces. We are one of the leading counties for numbers of suicides. And I believe that is all related to addiction. (Interview by author, Florida Keys, April 14)

Familiarity of Pastors with the Twelve Step Philosophy

Table 9. How Familiar Pastors Are with Twelve Step Format

	Yes	No	No Answer
Question 3: Attended Twelve Step Meeting?	74 percent (20)	26 percent (7)	0

	Strongly Agree	Somewhat Agree	Neutral/ No Opinion	Somewhat Disagree	Strongly Disagree	No Answer
Question 12: Familiar with Twelve Step Programs?	70 percent (19)	26 percent (7)	0	4 percent (1)	0	0

Note: Figures in parentheses are base numbers for the adjacent percentages.

As shown in Table 9, 74 percent of pastors reported having visited an open Twelve Step meeting, but 26 percent had never attended such a group. (For a graph of Twelve Step attendance, see Figure 4 below.) For this researcher, it was revealing to know that over a quarter had never attended such a Twelve Step group. Of pastors polled, 70 percent strongly agreed and 26 percent somewhat agreed that they were familiar with Twelve Step groups; in effect, 96 percent of clergy reported being familiar with Twelve Step programs. Pastors appeared enthusiastic and receptive to learning more on the subject.

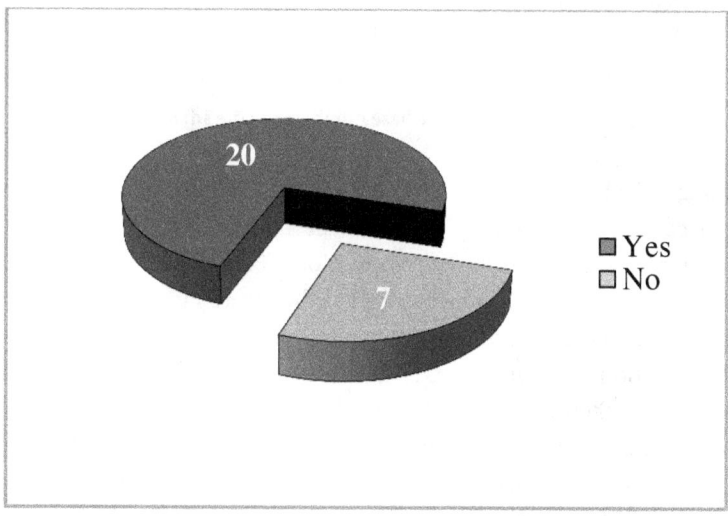

Figure 4. Attended a Twelve Step Meeting. Source: Survey, 2016.

In interviews, one clergyperson reflected that Twelve Step meetings were effective, but not as a stand-alone component. Another pastor confirmed the importance of Twelve Step groups: "One of the first things I check in with them on is the Twelve Steps, and I have found that the ones who are open to the Twelve Steps are actually easier to move toward recovery. The ones that . . . [are not] spiral down" (Interview by author, Florida Keys, April 8).

Awareness of Clergy of Christ-Centered Twelve Step Programs

Table 10. How Familiar Pastors Are with Christ-Centered Twelve Step Programs

	Strongly Agree	Somewhat Agree	Neutral/ No Opinion	Somewhat Disagree	Strongly Disagree	No Answer
Question 15: Familiar with Christ-Centered Twelve Step Programs?	48 percent (13)	33 percent (9)	7 percent (2)	0	11 percent (3)	0

Note: Figures in parentheses are base numbers for the adjacent percentages.

Although predominantly positive, the survey question on familiarity with Christ-centered Twelve Step programs in Table 10 reflected more diversity in responses than some other questions. Forty-eight percent strongly agreed and 33 percent somewhat agreed they were familiar, but 7 percent were neutral and 11 percent strongly disagreed. The dispersion of answers to this question was significant. Negative responses may be because Christ-based Twelve Step derivatives are relatively new—Celebrate Recovery, for example, was not founded until 1990. Negative answers reflected lack of familiarity, not necessarily disapproval. Almost one out of five frankly admitted lack of familiarity with them. Clearly, remedial education is needed on biblically-based Twelve Step programs.

Perceptions of Pastors About Church Members with Addictions

Table 11. Perceptions of Pastors about Church Members with Addictions

	Yes	No	No Answer
Question 6: Members of Church have Active Addictions?	74 percent (20)	22 percent (6)	4 percent (1)
Question 7: Members of Church Attend Twelve Step Groups?	82 percent (22)	15 percent (4)	4 percent (1)

Note: Figures in parentheses are base numbers for the adjacent percentages.

As Table 11 discloses, 22 percent of pastors felt that no members of their churches have active addictions, and approximately 15 percent did not know of parishioners who attend Twelve Step groups. One respondent elected "No Answer" for both questions, an option rarely exercised elsewhere in the survey. Nonetheless, 74 percent were aware that some members have active addictions, and 82 percent felt that some of their members attend Twelve Step meetings. Responses to these two questions were intriguing—a greater percentage of parishioners attend meetings than have active addictions. The sobering fact is that three out of four ministers still perceive that some members have active addictions. In an interview, one pastor described his interaction with addicts in this way:

> In general, I'll be happy to meet with them. My general rule is to meet with them three times. And in those three times, I'm going to evaluate whether I feel that pastoral counseling is adequate, or if it's just bigger than I can deal with... I would need to refer them to counseling, out-patient services, mental health services, whatever is appropriate.... When you go to war, you set the captives free and parade them through the city saying, "Our sons who were lost are now found." (Interview by author, Florida Keys, March 31)

THIRD GOAL: DETERMINING ATTITUDES OF CLERGY TOWARD THE TWELVE STEP MODEL

The third goal was to determine attitudes of clergy toward the Twelve Step model. The objectives of this goal were the following: to understand how favorable pastors are toward Twelve Step programs; to ascertain if clergy perceive addiction as a disease or a sin; to explore whether they see the Twelve Step formula as based on Christianity; to observe whether they think the Twelve Step mindset departs from Christian beliefs; and to determine whether pastors have a preference for Christ-centered Twelve Step programs.

Favorability Toward Twelve Step Programs?

Table 12. How Favorable Pastors Are Toward Twelve Step Programs

	Strongly Agree	Somewhat Agree	Neutral/ No Opinion	Somewhat Disagree	Strongly Disagree	No Answer
Question 13: Attitude Toward Twelve Step Programs Favorable?	85 percent (23)	11 percent (3)	4 percent (1)	0	0	0

Note: Figures in parentheses are base numbers for the adjacent percentages.

This question emerged as the core of the survey and reveals marked agreement in pastors viewing Twelve Step fellowships positively. Table 12 shows that 85 percent of clergy strongly agreed and 11 percent somewhat agreed that they were favorable toward Twelve Step programs. Responses were tightly grouped, and there was little variation in answers. The responses were overwhelming: 96 percent were strongly or somewhat favorable. Only one pastor registered neutral or no opinion. Based on feedback received by this writer several years before, the response to this question was not anticipated.

Endorsements for Twelve Step groups were also readily forthcoming from pastors in interviews who testified that they are "great," "fabulous," and "a lifeline." One minister declared, "I really admire the Twelve Step programs" (Interview by author, Florida Keys, April 14) and another exuded, "I'm a champion of addiction recovery in Twelve Steps" (Interview by author, Florida Keys, April 26). The group process of Twelve Step programs and the comradery in meetings impressed some pastors: "You could really sense that these folks depend on each other. . . . They had come to trust each other" (Interview by author, Florida Keys, March 31). A clergyperson claimed he always has the phone number in his office for a Twelve Step contact person. Another pastor consistently volunteered to go with parishioners to the first several Twelve Step meetings for moral support. One pastor explained: "The process of recovery from addiction can be very spiritual. Many of the folks who are involved in Twelve Step programs I have found to be in touch with their spiritual side quite often more than those who are not . . . I think Twelve Step programs really provide a good service in that way" (Interview by author, Florida Keys, April 11). Criticism of Twelve

Step groups was the exception rather than the rule. However, one pastor criticized participants in A.A. as being "stuck on the liturgy of the Twelve Steps. . . . I think it's possible for the Twelve Steps to be a replacement addiction. You stop being addicted to substances and start being addicted to the Twelve Steps" (Interview by author, Florida Keys, April 12).

Table 13. Attitude of Pastors Toward Those in Recovery from Addiction

	Strongly Agree	Somewhat Agree	Neutral/ No Opinion	Somewhat Disagree	Strongly Disagree	No Answer
Question 17: Those in Recovery Lead Christian Lives?	93 percent (25)	7 percent (2)	0	0	0	0
Question 18: Those in Recovery Welcome in Church?	100 percent (27)	0	0	0	0	0

Note: Figures in parentheses are base numbers for the adjacent percentages.

Answers presented in Table 13 were so one-sided, perhaps this researcher should have worded the questions differently. They reflected clergy attitudes that are virtually 100 percent favorable toward those in recovery. The level of agreement and acceptance was the highest of any question in the survey. Responses of clergy were unanimous toward those in addiction recovery being able to lead Christian lives and being accepted in churches. The research suggests that the prodigal will be welcomed home. One pastor spelled out these views in an interview:

> I think someone who goes through addiction or tremendous life changes or losses can find life massively reaffirmed on the other side of it. Those who are willing to deal with the pain and the struggle are able to find more meaning than they could have ever imagined. . . . In fact, they may become exemplary church members because they are capable of helping others in a way that non-recovering addicts can't. (Interview with author, Florida Keys, April 12)

Table 14. Outcomes of Pastors' Support of Twelve Step Groups

	Yes	No	No Answer
Question 4: Provide Space for Twelve Step Meetings in Past?	89 percent (24)	7 percent (2)	4 percent (1)
Question 5: Provide Space for Twelve Step Meetings Now?	44 percent (12)	48 percent (13)	7 percent (2)
Question 8: Encourage Members to Attend Twelve Step Programs?	93 percent (25)	4 percent (1)	4 percent (1)

Note: Figures in parentheses are base numbers for the adjacent percentages.

Table 14 demonstrates that 89 percent of pastors reported that their churches have provided space for Twelve Step meetings in the past, while 44 percent indicated that they currently provide meeting rooms. Ninety-three percent encouraged members in need to attend Twelve Step meetings. The results to these questions also exceeded expectations of this researcher. Nearly 90 percent have allowed Twelve Step use of their facilities in the past, and almost 45 percent currently provide meeting rooms. Virtually all pastors urged their parishioners to attend Twelve Step meetings. One minister stated in an interview that his church once had a problem with an A.A. group misusing their property and as a result, they no longer provide space for Twelve Step meetings. Another pastor, however, reported that her church has consistently hosted six Twelve Step meetings a week for over ten years. A clergyperson told of weekly meetings of Narcotics Anonymous held in his facility because it gives an endorsement and a statement of support. Another pastor offered a slightly different view, saying he supports a Celebrate Recovery group that meets off church grounds: "We do it in a neutral site on purpose. We never want anyone to be intimidated or feel that they can't . . . because it's on a church campus" (Interview by author, Florida Keys, April 14, 2016).

Research Evaluation

Addiction a Disease, Not a Sin?

Table 15. Addiction a Disease, Not a Sin

	Strongly Agree	Somewhat Agree	Neutral/ No Opinion	Somewhat Disagree	Strongly Disagree	No Answer
Question 11: Is Addiction a Disease, Not a Sin?	37 percent (10)	26 percent (7)	4 percent (1)	19 percent (5)	15 percent (4)	0

Note: Figures in parentheses are base numbers for the adjacent percentages.

This question produced the greatest divergence of opinion in the survey, as is represented in Table 15. Discounting the single neutral response, 63 percent strongly agreed or somewhat agreed that addiction is a disease and 34 percent somewhat disagreed or strongly disagreed and consider it a sin. The spread of answers for this question was the largest in the survey. (For a graph on whether clergy see addiction as a disease or a sin, see Figure 5 below.) The relationship between sin and disease in the addiction model is discussed in the chapters on theology and literature review. In the response to this survey question, however, this relationship becomes more tangible. Asked to make a choice, pastors are divided, two-thirds preferring the disease concept and one-third favoring the sin explanation. In retrospect, a follow-up question was needed asking if pastors felt addiction could be both sin and disease. In an interview, at least one pastor stipulated that addiction is not "either-or," but "both-and" (Interview by author, Florida Keys, March 31).

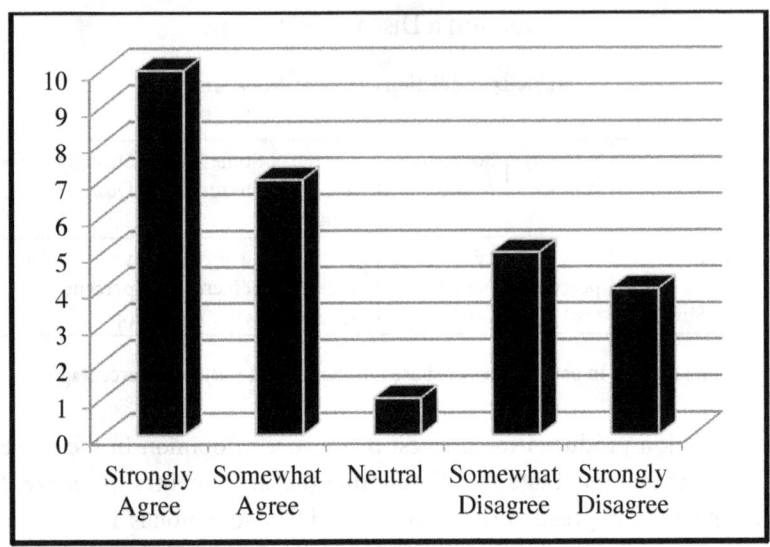

Figure 5. Addiction a Disease, Not a Sin. Source: Survey, 2016.

In interviews, pastors sometimes commented on the nature of sin. One minister suggested, "If you define sin as breaking relationship with God, then I can see that . . . [addiction] breaks that relationship" (Interview by author, Florida Keys, April 14). A rabbi offered this perspective: "[Jewish texts say] 'no one sins unless it's insanity'. . . . There's another sense of sin in the Jewish tradition, it means to 'miss the mark.' It's actually an archery term. . . . You've gone in the wrong direction to some degree" (Interview by author, Florida Keys, April 11). Another minister agreed: "Sin is where we come up short of what God has destined for our lives" (Interview by author, Florida Keys, April 26). One pastor emphasized the sin aspect of addiction: "Some people have forfeited their choices by continual submission and find themselves in the full grasp of Satan. We're dealing with what I call a great conflict between Christ and Satan" (Interview by author, Florida Keys, April 6). Another minister interviewed stressed the disease aspect:

> It's a disease and I think it's also genetic. I think it's something people don't have any control over. And just like if you have diabetes, you have any kind of sickness, it's something you have no control over, and you have to seek assistance in order to be able to rectify it and be able to move forward in a positive way. (Interview by author, Florida Keys, April 4)

Finally, in interviews there were those who felt addiction is both. A clergyperson asserted, "It's a disease that can become a sin" (Interview by author, Florida Keys, April 8). Another suggested that it is a combination of sin and disease:

> I somewhat disagree that it's a disease and not a sin because it's "both-and." I don't think it's an either-or question. . . . It's a sin to have any other God before him, however, I think I'm pretty clear on the mental health issues that are directly related to it, and so I think it needs to be treated differently than some other things. (Interview by author, Florida Keys, March 31)

Twelve Steps Based Upon Christianity?

Table 16. Twelve Steps Based Upon Christianity

	Strongly Agree	Somewhat Agree	Neutral/ No Opinion	Somewhat Disagree	Strongly Disagree	No Answer
Question 14: Twelve Steps Based Upon Christianity?	33 percent (9)	33 percent (9)	15 percent (4)	15 percent (4)	4 percent (1)	0

Note: Figures in parentheses are base numbers for the adjacent percentages.

Table 16 reveals that clergy had a significant difference of opinion on whether the Twelve Steps are based upon Christianity. Sixty-six percent strongly agreed or somewhat agreed that they are, while 34 percent strongly disagreed, somewhat disagreed or were neutral. The distribution of responses to this question was one of the largest recorded in the survey. (For a graph on whether clergy see the Twelve Steps as based upon Christianity, see Figure 6 below.)

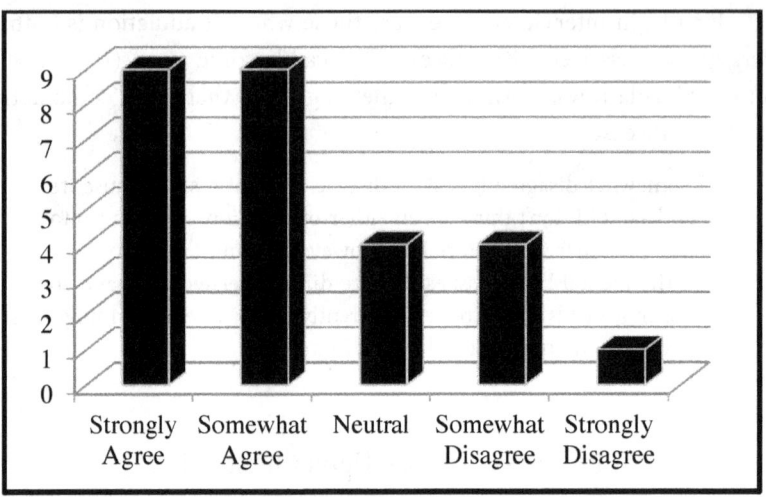

Figure 6. Twelve Steps Based Upon Christianity. Source: Survey, 2016.

In interviews, one clergyperson recalled that although non-denominational, the Twelve Step strategy originated with Christians and has a Christian base. Another pastor observed that Twelve Step groups are transformative, but have an open theology. Finally, a pastor concluded:

> I think in general the ideals are Christian in origin though there are times when either the group or individuals don't necessarily follow a Christian world-view but adapt it to their life. A lot has to do with their leadership, too. The more the leadership is overtly or strongly Christian the more likely that carries through to the group. . . . I think God works through Twelve Step groups. (Interview by author, Florida Keys, March 31)

Twelve Step Mindset Departs from Christian Beliefs?

As has been seen in Table 16, 19 percent of pastors somewhat disagreed or strongly disagreed that the Twelve Steps are based on Christianity. In interviews, some clergy had reservations about the emphasis of the Twelve Steps upon a Higher Power, instead of the "one and only saving Christ" (Interview by author, Florida Keys, April 6). One minister argued:

> There are some Twelve Step programs who have taken the Lord out of it. . . . As they were originally established, I believe the Twelve

> Step programs were great, Christ-centered, and so on. Now you can have a tree or anything else for your Higher Power.... A lot of addiction is of a spiritual nature, and needs spiritual warfare.... In many cases, the deliverance of Christ can go beyond [what the world offers]. That's one of the few problems I've got with the programs. (Interview by author, Florida Keys, April 8)

Another pastor, however, acknowledged the difference in roles between Twelve Step groups and churches:

> I know that there are plenty of Christian clergy who have difficulty with it, but I don't see any competition with it whatsoever.... if you're seeking Higher Power the only Higher Power that exists is God.... [The Twelve Steps] purpose isn't to teach religion; their purpose is to activate a person's faith. It's the church's purpose to teach religion. The Twelve Step [programs] have never claimed to be a church. (Interview by author, Florida Keys, April 8)

Responses show that two-thirds felt that the Twelve Steps are based on Christianity and one-third disagreed or were unsure. This disparity should not be surprising. Historical research reported earlier indicates that A.A. had discernible roots in Christian churches, but this was almost a century ago, and churches have since distanced and often disassociated themselves.

Preference for Christ-Centered Twelve Step Programs?

Table 17. Attitude of Pastors toward Christ-Centered Programs

	Strongly Agree	Somewhat Agree	Neutral/ No Opinion	Somewhat Disagree	Strongly Disagree	No Answer
Question 15: Familiar with Christ-Centered Programs?	48 percent (13)	33 percent (9)	7 percent (2)	0	11 percent (3)	0
Question 16: Attitude Toward Christ-Centered Programs Favorable?	67 percent (18)	26 percent (7)	7 percent (2)	0	0	0

Note: Figures in parentheses are base numbers for the adjacent percentages.

Attitudes toward Christ-centered Twelve Step programs were positive, as is summarized in Table 17, with 93 percent strongly agreeing or somewhat agreeing that they were favorable. Interestingly, those who recorded being familiar with them was somewhat lower at 81 percent. These findings included responses of a Jewish rabbi and a Unitarian minister in the group polled. Interviews also reflected that there were pastors who were unfamiliar with Christ-centered programs, but who were favorable nevertheless. As one clergyperson admitted, "I would be [favorable] if there are Twelve Step programs that center on Christ. I don't know about them personally, but I would be in favor of them, anything that would place Christ in the center" (Interview by author, Florida Keys, April 6). However, another pastor emphasized discretion in referring members to Christ-centered programs:

> There are some individuals that I would recommend A.A. as the Twelve Step program, depending on where a person is in their spiritual journey. There are others I would recommend straight to a Celebrate Recovery program. . . . If a person is still trying to discover the reality of God, and they are in that vague ground of Higher Power as something bigger than they are, then A.A. [would be best]. (Interview by author, Florida Keys, April 14)

To summarize, responses to questions pertaining to Christ-centered Twelve Step programs were positive, although something of an enigma. As reported above, almost 95 percent of pastors were favorable, but only 80 percent reported they were familiar with them. In the nature of a semantic response, approximately 15 percent who were not familiar with Christ-centered programs nevertheless had a bias toward "anything that would place Christ in the center" (Interview by author, Florida Keys, April 6).

FOURTH GOAL: HOW RESEARCH INFORMS THE OUTCOME OF A COURSE SYLLABUS FOR TRAINING CLERGY

The fourth goal of this study was the outcome of a course syllabus for clergy and those in ministerial training on addiction and the Twelve Step method. The first objective of this goal was to evaluate whether the research in this study adequately informed the proposed syllabus. This afforded the opportunity to reflect further on what the statistics mean. The field research indicated that history of addiction in pastors' families is significant. It may well play a role in shaping their attitudes and priorities, and thus should be included in the syllabus. Eighty-nine percent of those surveyed strongly

Research Evaluation

agreed that there was a background of addiction in their families. To help pastors understand the impact of this history, the proposed syllabus should include a review of family background, and a detailed genogram of their family tree, with family members clearly identified who suffered from addiction (see section II.A of the syllabus outline in Appendix G). A recurring theme in both surveys and interviews was how widespread and significant the problem of addiction is, not only in the Florida Keys, but in society in general. The proposed syllabus should help clergy better understand addiction (see section II.B of the syllabus outline in Appendix G).

The survey showed that 70 percent of pastors strongly agreed that they are familiar with Twelve Step programs, and another 26 percent somewhat agreed. The proposed syllabus should build upon this foundation by including background and fundamentals of Twelve Step practice (see sections II.C and II.D of the syllabus outline in Appendix G). Field research also reflected, however, that over one-quarter of the pastors have never attended a Twelve Step meeting. The syllabus and course should include provision for visitation to open Twelve Step groups and evaluation by ministers (see section II.D.3 of the syllabus outline in Appendix G). Field research reflected less familiarity of ministers with Christ-based Twelve Step programs than with Twelve Step groups in general. This question had one of the largest deviation of responses in the survey. Nevertheless, attitudes toward Christ-centered groups were very positive, with 93 percent of pastors strongly agreeing or somewhat agreeing that they were favorable. A syllabus and course for pastors need to increase understanding by clergy of such groups (see section II.D.2 of the syllabus outline in Appendix G).

Surveys and interviews confirmed that pastors are virtually 100 percent favorable toward Twelve Step programs. This was perhaps the single most positive outcome of the survey, with one of the smallest variation of answers of any question. The field research did not uphold the assumption made in chapter 1 of this book, that clergy "may have unfavorable attitudes toward Twelve Step methodology." The survey showed that 93 percent of pastors encouraged members suffering from addiction to attend Twelve Step meetings. This is, therefore, an opportune time to develop a syllabus for pastors and those in ministerial training on addiction recovery through Twelve Step philosophy (see section II of the syllabus outline in Appendix G).

The greatest difference of opinion of responses in the survey centered on the question of whether addiction is a disease or a sin. As noted, this had the largest distribution of answers to any question, with 63 percent feeling that addiction is a disease, and 34 percent considering it a sin. A syllabus and course for clergy need to address this critical issue in which science and theology meet (see section II.E.1.a of the syllabus outline in Appendix G).

Another subject of the survey that reflected disagreement among pastors was whether the Twelve Steps are based upon Christianity, with 66 percent feeling that they are, and 34 percent being neutral or disagreeing. Results were loosely grouped. Through interviews, some clergy expressed strong reservations about the Twelve Step emphasis upon a Higher Power, as opposed to the Christian concept of God and the traditional role of Christ. A syllabus and course for ministerial training need to respond to these issues and explore the historical roots of the Twelve Step movement and its relationship to Christianity (see sections II.C, II.E.1, and II.E.2 of the syllabus outline in Appendix G).

Finally, the survey indicated that 44 percent of the churches represented provided space for Twelve Step meetings, and 93 percent of pastors encouraged members to attend Twelve Step programs. In addition to providing space and encouragement, a syllabus for training pastors should further clarify the support of clergy through Fifth Step ministries, preaching, and facilitating Christ-centered Twelve Step groups in particular (see section II.E.3 of the syllabus outline in Appendix G).

A GENERAL NARRATIVE OF WHAT PASTORS SHARED

The heart of the research was the interviews and what ministers confided about their understanding and hope for addiction recovery. Since the first impression given to this researcher over twenty years ago, their views have changed and grown. Most are now deeply concerned about the problem of addiction and almost all are in favor of the Twelve Step approach.

One pastor, for example, impressed this writer with how comfortable and at ease he felt with Twelve Step programs. He sat on the other side of his desk with his legs crossed, and leaned back with his hands behind his head. He reminisced about attending A.A. meetings in his church:

> My opinion is favorable.... Not only the principles, but the support of the group. The interaction with others who are dealing with the same thing makes a big difference.... I think God works through Twelve Step groups, but uses that means to point people to the relationships they need to deal with their addictions. (Interview by author, Florida Keys, March 31)

Research Evaluation

He went on to confess how difficult it has been in the past to address addiction in churches: "In the community [addiction is] . . . pretty big and invasive. We just hide it better. We've learned you're not supposed to say that stuff in church. . . . In church it's there; we just don't admit it as much" (Interview by author, Florida Keys, March 31). Another cleric who has a passion for combatting addiction, spoke of the importance of churches taking risks and going outside their comfort zone:

> There are hurting people everywhere. . . . People who need churches to be creative and daring, and go outside of their comfort zone. There are many churches and pastors who will say, "We're outside of our comfort zone," and who are being risky and opening up a Twelve Step program in their church. . . . Risky is inviting those [people] into your church family and setting and allowing yourself to sit with the broken and outcast. (Interview by author, Florida Keys, March 31)

The next minister shared how committed he is to counselling those who are troubled by addiction. As he said, "I would share of my own struggles with addiction that has been in my family, and would then clearly try to get them to attend meetings, Twelve Step meetings" (Interview by author, Florida Keys, April 4). A clergyperson with a similar background told of growing up "in an alcoholic family, so I was a member of Alanon for years" (Interview by author, Florida Keys, April 8). This cleric disclosed:

> [Addiction's] been a part of my life since the day I was born. My father was an alcoholic. He died because of his alcoholism. He was horribly abusive. . . . That gives me a particular foundation. The area I chose to focus on was domestic violence, rather than addiction. (Interview by author, Florida Keys, April 8)

When asked about referring church members to Twelve Step groups, this individual declared, "I don't see any competition with it whatsoever. . . . I believe whether you call God 'God' or not, God is God" (Interview by author, Florida Keys, April 8).

A pastor who participated in many interventions reported the following: "I've had some success in getting people to admit it, and go to Twelve Step programs. I've had some success in getting people to go to a medical doctor. And I've also been told to 'shut up and get out of my life'" (Interview by author, Florida Keys, April 11). Another minister spoke fondly of visiting Twelve Step meetings. As he said, "It was wonderful. . . . I was so very warmly received. . . . They are not a know-all and an end-all, but they are very important for many people, and they are a life-line" (Interview by author, Florida Keys, April 11). Yet another pastor testified to the change and development that takes place in the Twelve Step process: "I think sometimes people go through the Twelve Steps and return to serve their faith community, and find that they've moved on and that the faith community has not.... When they return to a community that is often judgmental or silent, they don't feel they can sit there authentically" (Interview by author, Florida Keys, April 12). A different clergyperson commented on the openness and opportunity for personal growth in Twelve Step groups:

> When my son was having severe issues and I didn't know what to do, I went to Alanon.... It changed our relationship in a positive way and eventually it changed his way of being ... There are universal values that are woven into the Twelve Step program, but I don't think you have to be a Christian to be involved.... I think regardless of where you are, you are still welcome in a Twelve Step program. (Interview by author, Florida Keys, April 14)

One of the most compelling testimonials came from an individual who was flexible enough to recognize that if he took a prospect to Celebrate Recovery, the newcomer "might feel this is 'just a little too over the top for me, a little too religious'.... [Instead he would] take them by the hand and take them to A.A., or find a sponsor." Moreover, he felt Twelve Step groups are "essential. Absolutely essential." His response to a newcomer is, "We've got to get you to a Twelve Step program right away" (Interview by author, Florida Keys, April 14). The last pastor to be cited stated that he has "benefited from ... [the Twelve Steps] in seasons of my life." As he recalled, "I did a three month sermon series on the Twelve Steps ... [which was] excellent, probably one of the best series in terms of acceptance" (Interview by author, Florida Keys, April 26).

SUMMARY

The current chapter has evaluated the research in terms of its fulfilling the initial goals of this study: understanding pre-conditions of pastors' views, ascertaining how informed pastors are about addiction and the Twelve Step format, determining attitudes of clergy toward the Twelve Step model, and considering how the research informs the outcome of a course syllabus for training clergy. Finally, this chapter reconstructed a general narrative of the stories that pastors shared.

Chapter 6

Development of a Syllabus

THE FOURTH GOAL OF this study was the outcome of a course syllabus for clergy and those in ministerial training on addiction recovery through Twelve Step philosophy. The previous chapter ended by considering the first objective of this goal, whether the research in this study adequately informed the proposed syllabus. This chapter focuses on the second objective, the development of a syllabus that included the following: preconditions that influence views and susceptibility to addiction; a greater knowledge base on addictionology; history and background of the Twelve Steps; familiarity with how Twelve Step organizations work; and spiritual features of the Twelve Step design and its relationship to Christianity. Before considering the syllabus, however, it is appropriate to review seminary courses in addiction recovery.

SURVEY OF EXISTING COURSES

As noted in the chapter on contemporary literature, the National Center on Addiction and Substance Abuse at Columbia University conducted a survey of seminary courses on addiction. Only 25.8 percent of seminary presidents reported that students were required to take addiction courses (National Center on Addiction 2001, 3). In the research of the current study, none of the pastors interviewed reported taking a course in addiction recovery, and none could recall if their seminaries offered such a class. Consequently, this writer felt compelled to do at least some informal research on the current availability of such courses. He contacted twelve seminaries judged *likely* to have courses in addiction recovery. Only four offer such classes, typically under the auspices of pastoral counseling.

- In 1985, the Methodist Theological School in Delaware, Ohio (MTSO) initiated an M.A. in Alcoholism and Drug Abuse Ministry. In 1998, this program transitioned to an M.A. in Counseling Ministries with a Track in Addiction Counseling. This two-year program now includes the following courses not only in counseling, but also on the spiritual and theological dimensions of recovery: PC 555, Introduction to Chemical Dependency Ministries; PC 655, Alcoholism and Other Addiction Counseling; PC 756, Spiritual Dimension of Illness and Recovery; and CT 659, Gender, Sin, and Addiction, the latter taught by Linda A. Mercadante.

- The Christian Theological Seminary in Indianapolis offers the following elective course, which deals with attitudes towards addicts and addiction, and experience with Twelve Step programs: P 650, Treating Addictive Behavior, currently offered every other year.

- The Fuller Theological Seminary in Pasadena has a sequence in Recovery Ministry in both its MDiv and MA programs, which includes the following courses: CN 553, Pastoral Care and Abuse; CN 567, Spiritual Formation and the Twelve Steps; EV 532, Recovery Ministry in the Local Church; and an elective such as CN 557, Pastoral Care and Addictions.

- Finally, the Wesley Seminary at Indiana Wesleyan University presents the following courses in addiction, which give an overview of substance abuse and behavioral disorders such as gambling and sexual addiction: CNS 511, Issues in Addiction Recovery; and CNS 545, Counseling and Addicted Families.

As previously mentioned, the National Association for Children of Alcoholics (NACOA) asked Robert H. Albers, former editor of the *Journal of Ministry in Addiction & Recovery*, to write a curriculum titled *Addiction and the Family: A Seminary Curriculum* (2012). The NACOA curriculum does not contain a publication date, but "it was made available in 2012" (Robert H. Albers, email to author, April 26, 2016). The modules of the NACOA course address attitudes, awareness, assimilation, and action. Particularly suited for self-study, it appears to be a comprehensive and practical curriculum.

To summarize, as of 2001 the National Center on Addiction and Substance Abuse at Columbia University showed merely 25 percent of seminaries required addiction courses, and informal research by this writer in 2016 revealed that only 33 percent of seminaries polled offer classes in

Development of a Syllabus

addiction recovery. The reality is that most seminaries still do not have even an entry-level course on this subject. Informed by the field research reported in the last chapter, this writer proposes the following syllabus for pastors and those in ministerial training on addiction recovery through Twelve Step philosophy.

THE SYLLABUS FOR A COURSE

The goal of the proposed course is to increase understanding and support by pastors and those in ministerial training of addiction recovery through Twelve Step philosophy. For an outline of the syllabus for teaching, see Appendix G.[1] In a final syllabus, topics in this chapter and the outline would need to be assigned specific dates according to the number and length of class meetings.

Educational Objectives

As a result of completing this course, participants will:

- Be aware of preconditions that influence views on and susceptibility to addiction
- Develop a knowledge base of current thinking on addictionology
- Become informed about the history and background of the Twelve Steps
- Become familiar with how the Twelve Step programs work; in particular, Alcoholics Anonymous and Celebrate Recovery
- Understand the spiritual features of the Twelve Step design and its relationship to Christianity

Course Content Areas

First, preconditions that influence views on and susceptibility to addiction will be studied, including the genetics of addiction and the history of addiction in families, which will incorporate designing a genogram. Second, current thinking on addictionology will be reviewed. This vital area will view addiction as a social and cultural problem, a neurobiological phenomena,

---

1. The outline of the syllabus is also available online (Hudson 2016b).

and a syndrome or spectrum disorder including both substance and behavior or process addictions. Major characteristics of addiction will be considered including the following:

- Loss of willpower and control
- Denial
- Tolerance
- Withdrawal
- Substitution/Reformation

Third, the history and background of the Twelve Step movement will be discussed, encompassing Temperance and Prohibition; the Oxford Group and Christian origins of A.A.; the co-founders of A.A. (Bill Wilson and Dr. Bob Smith); and the literature of A.A., such as *Alcoholics Anonymous* (Alcoholics Anonymous World Services 2001) and *Twelve Steps and Twelve Traditions* (Alcoholics Anonymous World Services 2011). Fourth, how Twelve Step programs work will be explored, taking into account the Twelve Steps and the Twelve Traditions of A.A. In addition, attention will be given to Celebrate Recovery's Twelve Steps with Scripture Comparisons and the Eight Principles based upon the Sermon on the Mount. Visitation at open A.A. and C.R. meetings will be a priority.

Fifth, the spiritual features of the Twelve Step design and its relationship to Christianity will be examined, involving such questions as whether the Twelve Steps are based upon Christianity, whether addiction is a disease or a sin, and if the Twelve Steps depart from Christianity. Theological issues surveyed will include the concept of God and a Higher Power, the character of Christ (i.e. in Celebrate Recovery), the role of prayer and miracles, and fellowship as spiritual community. Finally, specific roles for clergy will be identified such as sponsorship and Fifth Step ministry, counseling and referral, preaching effectively on addiction recovery, allocating meeting space for Twelve Step groups, and facilitating Christ-centered Twelve Step programs.

Assignments

There will be a pre-course paper on students' views toward addiction, and the phenomena and social problems of addiction. The assigned length will be 8–10 pages and it will comprise 30 percent of the grade. There will be a post-course paper on the history and background of the Twelve Steps, how they work, the spiritual features of the Twelve Step model, and its relationship to Christianity. The assigned length will be 18–20 pages, and it will represent 60 percent of the grade. Finally, class participation, including visitation reports of open A.A. and C.R. meetings, will account for 10 percent of the grade.

Course Bibliography

A bibliography for the syllabus will include the following references:

Alcoholics Anonymous World Services. 1957. *Alcoholics Anonymous Comes of Age: A Brief History of A.A.*

———. 2001. *Alcoholics Anonymous: The Story of How Many Thousands of Men and Women Have Recovered from Alcoholism.*

———. 2011. *Twelve Steps and Twelve Traditions.*

American Psychiatric Association. 2013. *Diagnostic and Statistical Manual of Mental Disorders (DSM-5).*

Baker, John. 2012a. *Celebrate Recovery: Stepping out of Denial and Into God's Grace.*

———. 2012b. *Celebrate Recovery: Taking an Honest and Spiritual Inventory.*

———. 2012c. *Celebrate Recovery: Getting Right with God, Yourself, and Others.*

———. 2012d. *Celebrate Recovery: Growing with Christ While Helping Others.*

Gabriel, Gregory P. 1993. "How Do You Hear a Fifth Step?" *Journal of Ministry in Addiction & Recovery.*

Kurtz, Ernest. 1991. *Not-God: A History of Alcoholics Anonymous.*

Latcovich, Mark A. 1995. "The Clergyperson and the Fifth Step." *Journal of Ministry in Addiction and Chemical Dependency Treatment.*

May, Gerald G. 1991. *Addiction & Grace: Love and Spirituality in the Healing of Addictions.*

Mercadante, Linda A. 1996. *Victims & Sinners: Spiritual Roots of Addiction and Recovery.*

Ries, Richard K., David A. Fiellin, Shannon C. Miller, and Richard Saitz, eds. 2014. *The ASAM Principles of Addiction Medicine.*

White, William L. 2014. *Slaying the Dragon: The History of Addiction Treatment and Recovery in America.*

SUMMARY

This chapter provided a brief survey of existing seminary courses on addiction recovery. It also addressed the second objective of the fourth goal of this study, the outcome of a course syllabus for clergy and those in ministerial training on addiction recovery through Twelve Step philosophy. The syllabus centers on preconditions that influence views and susceptibility to addiction, a knowledge base on addictionology, history and background of the Twelve Step movement, how Twelve Step organizations work, and the spiritual features of the Twelve Step design and its relationship to

Christianity, including specific roles for clergy. It is this writer's hope that this course syllabus will become an actual outcome and be utilized by seminaries in both MDiv and DMin programs. To that end, it would be appropriate to have this syllabus peer-reviewed by professional educators and certified addictionologists.

Chapter 7

Conclusion

As this study draws to a close, it is fitting to summarize some of its chief findings. Addiction has a widespread and devastating impact on our society. It costs more than four hundred billion dollars a year in lost productivity, crime, and health care. Addiction has been increasingly transferred from treatment programs to the criminal justice system and has resulted in the imprisonment of four times the number of people incarcerated in 1980. It has an inequitable impact on people of color.

For over two hundred years, our country has witnessed various interventions ranging from the Temperance Movement to the Washingtonian Society, from the Emmanuel Movement to the Oxford Group. The roots of Alcoholics Anonymous were in the Emmanuel Movement and the Oxford Group, but it was a direct "spin-off" from the Oxford Group. The six principles of the Oxford Group became the basis of the Twelve Steps of A.A.

Churches have vacillated in their role: They supported Temperance and Prohibition, then distanced themselves and abdicated leadership in post-Repeal America. A handful of clergy were faithful in their early support of Alcoholics Anonymous, including Samuel M. Shoemaker, Harry Emerson Fosdick, Walter F. Tunks, Dilworth Lipton, Edward Dowling, and Sister Ignatia. Not until the end of the twentieth century, however, did churches begin to reconcile themselves to the Twelve Step initiative with the advent of Christ-centered programs such as Celebrate Recovery.

Theological and biblical perspectives have considered humanity's limitations; God's omnipotence, abundance and forgiveness; Christ's healing role; the place of prayer and miracles; and the function of fellowship and community. Addiction is about human imperfection, and human imperfection has traditionally been about sin as well as disease. Sin has been considered from Manichean, Pelagian, and Augustine perspectives. Today sin is not so much about specific behaviors as about general attitudes, orientation, and direction; it is a "turning away from that to which one belongs" (Tillich 1967, 2:46). The position of this writer is that addiction may begin as a sinful choice, but then transforms into disease, complete with neurochemical attributes. The answer to sin, whether from the perspective of tradition or that of addiction, is God—his omnipotence, abundance and generosity, and especially his forgiveness and the opportunity for a second chance. Christ had a special affinity with those who are afflicted and suffer, and is an inspiring symbol of healing. The mystery of prayer is response to the *One* who is remote, yet is as close as our heartbeat. Life has always been a miracle, and it is filled with countless miracles, including that of recovery from addiction. In the vastness of the universe, men and women are created as creatures who belong, who love, and who are healed in community.

The review of contemporary literature has been an exciting venture into the sources of our knowledge on addiction and the Twelve Step process. First, the literature review has showed us as pastors what we do not know, what our knowledge deficiencies are. Remarkably, two different studies came to the same conclusion. The Substance Abuse and Mental Health Administration reported that few schools of theology offer instruction on addiction. Likewise, the National Center on Addiction and Substance Abuse found that only 12.5 percent of pastors receive training on this subject. Second, review of the literature disclosed the background of Twelve Step programs: the role of Benjamin Rush, the Temperance Movement, the works of Richard Peabody and the Emmanuel Movement. It included literature about the Oxford Group and studies on Alcoholics Anonymous, notably by Ernest Kurtz and William L. White.

Third, the literature review reflecting how Twelve Step organizations function emphasized A.A. literature, including *Alcoholics Anonymous* (Alcoholics Anonymous World Services 2001), *Twelve Steps and Twelve Traditions* (Alcoholics Anonymous World Services 2011), and other ancillary publications. The four editions of the *Big Book* have kept its first one hundred sixty-four pages intact. After the first printing, minor changes were made, including the wording of the Twelfth Step and the addition of Appendix II on spirituality. In each of the editions, individual stories comprising the second half of the book were changed to reflect characteristics of current membership. *Twelve Steps and Twelve Traditions* was reviewed as offering insight into sobriety and good living, for example,

Conclusion

in its discussion of relationships as sometimes involving distortions of domination or over-dependence on others. Other publications considered were *Daily Reflections* (Alcoholics Anonymous World Services 1990), *The A.A. Way of Life* (Alcoholics Anonymous World Services 1967), and *Living Sober* (Alcoholics Anonymous World Services 1975b).

Literature review on how Twelve Step organizations work also included the curriculum of Celebrate Recovery, the Christ-centered Twelve Step program authored by John Baker and Rick Warren. The four basic texts of Celebrate Recovery are *Stepping Out of Denial Into God's Grace* (Baker 2012a), *Taking an Honest and Spiritual Inventory* (Baker 2012b), *Getting Right with God, Yourself, and Others* (Baker 2012c), and *Growing in Christ While Helping Others* (Baker 2012d). Founded at the Saddleback Church, Celebrate Recovery utilizes the Twelve Steps of A.A., with the First Step expanded to include many addictions and compulsive behaviors. In addition to alcohol, the C.R. program provides for recovery from anger, chemical dependency, abuse, sexual addiction, and love and relationship addiction. Supplementing the Steps, Celebrate Recovery presents Eight Principles based on the Sermon on the Mount. The Third Principle calls for C.R. members to commit their lives and wills to Christ's care and control. Grace Methodist Church in Fort Myers, Florida, is a prominent example of one of the twenty-nine thousand churches that offer this program. As Pastor Jose Acevedo of Grace Methodist observes, "Many churches . . . offer people Jesus the Healer without offering healing ministries" (Swanson and McBean 2011, 109).

Fourth, the review of contemporary literature included works on the spirituality of the Twelve Steps. Here multiple authors were identified, including Michael Hardin and Linda Mercadante, the latter writing extensively on sin and addiction. The connection between the Twelve Steps and Christian ministry has been fixed in place by E. Morton Jellinek, Howard J. Clinebell Jr., and Robert H. Albers. Gerald G. May entered the dialogue with his significant but unorthodox crossover work on addiction and grace. An alternative view of the spirituality of the Twelve Steps was acknowledged, including the dissenting voices of Herbert Fingarette, William L. Playfair, and Martin and Deidre Bobgan.

Fifth, the literature review included state-of-the-art studies on addiction theory, including the writing of William R. Miller, works of the American Psychiatric Association (*DSM-5*) and the American Society of Addiction Medicine (ASAM). Addiction has been observed as having consistent characteristics, evolutionary roots, a neurobiological base, and qualifies as a spectrum disorder. Workshops in South Florida presented by Dr. Eugene L. Manuel and Dr. John C. Eustace provided deep background for the literature review. In addition, this researcher had an opportunity to participate by presenting a paper on "Resilience in Addiction Recovery" at the Miami Baptist Hospital symposium on February 28, 2015. Sixth, the review of the contemporary literature has considered the realm of addiction treatment, accessing the works of sociologist Robin Room, Marty Mann, E. Morton Jellinek, and William L. White, and including William R. Miller and Stephen Rollnick's contribution of Motivational Interviewing.

Field research consisted of surveys and interviews of clergy in the Florida Keys (Monroe County), an area heavily impacted by addiction. This study surveyed 42 percent and interviewed 22 percent of pastors in Monroe County. Conducting the research was a challenging and moving experience, both in gathering the data and getting to know other pastors better. The purpose of the research was to determine demographics, knowledgeability, and attitudes of pastors on not only traditional Twelve Step groups but Christ-centered programs as well. The most recent feedback to this researcher was a number of years ago when many clergy were not favorable toward the Twelve Step process and some opposed groups such as A.A. The last few years have wrought significant changes in their hearts and minds. Confounding one of the assumptions of this study, research reveals that remarkable unanimity now exists among ministers in their approval and support of Twelve Step activity. However, clergy frequently lack familiarity and understanding of the dynamics of the Twelve Step process. Over one quarter of the pastors have never been to a Twelve Step meeting. As this research progressed, many ministers have asked to have a copy of the results. The Upper Keys Ministerial Association has requested workshops on the topic, and is considering making addiction ministry and education one of its central objectives. This is an auspicious time for designing and promoting a course for pastors and those in ministerial training on addiction recovery through Twelve Step philosophy. It should be emphasized that the current research is designed for replication in other locations, and specific guidelines for reproducing the study are given.

The preceding chapter briefly reviewed existing seminary courses and presented the content for a syllabus on addiction recovery through Twelve Step philosophy for those in ministerial training. Inasmuch as possible, it covers all goals and knowledge objectives discussed in this study. If in practice it proves too long for a three-hour course, it could be consolidated or taught as more than one course. The syllabus is offered to seminaries and theological schools for their use—this writer is eager to support such efforts, either by teaching or serving as a consultant.

LESSONS LEARNED

It is said that as the author writes the book, the book writes the author. This study affected this writer in a number of ways. Initially, he approached the problem of addiction solely from the perspective of traditional or secular Twelve Step programs such as A.A. or N.A. He came to realize that this was not consistent with the reality and success of Christianized Twelve Step groups including Celebrate Recovery. Christ-centered programs offer a viable alternative, one that some pastors and churches may find especially appealing. Hopefully those reading this study will not be limited by such a bias, and will be equally open to both traditional and non-traditional Twelve Step options.

Another way this writer expanded his view was in his understanding of the sin-disease dichotomy of addiction. He was predisposed to favoring the disease concept, and did not acknowledge the sin aspect of addiction. Due to researching this book, he has modified his perception and now acknowledges the viability of sin at the beginning of the addiction process, with disease dominating as the syndrome progresses. Readers of this study are likewise encouraged to be open-minded on this subject. If, for example, they are now predisposed primarily to a sin model of addiction, perhaps they will become more receptive to the disease aspect.

A further way this project influenced this researcher was in acceptance of the role of contemporary addiction theory. Initially, this writer felt that the field of neurobiology was so technical that it should be reserved for scientists and addictionologists. He had to overcome that preconception, and recognize that just as religion has much to say to science, so science may have something to say to religion. Hopefully, those reading this study will arrive at that conclusion sooner.

A final yet most significant way this study influenced this writer was in the relationship to his fellow pastors in the Florida Keys. As the project began, they were thought of simply as survey participants or interviewees. Particularly as interviews got underway, this perspective changed. Fellow clergy were much more than research subjects—they became confidants and friends. Sitting across the table, they became real. They had parents, brothers and sisters, wives and husbands, children and friends who struggled with addiction. All too often, their loved ones lost that battle. These pastors disclosed their vulnerability, their trust, and their courage. Most important, they shared their witness to the providence of God. In conducting research of this type, this writer learned how vital it is to have the human connection—to rely not only on anonymous surveys, but to include personal interaction. Ultimately, this study has to be dedicated to my fellow clergy, for their insight and faithfulness.

AFTERWORD

God is in calm and quiet, but he is also in the storm. He is in the depths of addiction when we experience what Saint John of the Cross describes as the "dark night of the soul" (John of the Cross 2003). Yet, as the *Big Book* says, "God does not make too hard terms with those who seek Him. . . . the Realm of the Spirit is broad, roomy, all inclusive; never exclusive or forbidding to those who earnestly seek" (Alcoholics Anonymous World Services 2001, 46).

Those who suffer from addiction learn the truth of what Gerald May discloses, "We were never meant to be completely satisfied" (May 1991, 180). As Augustine confesses, "Our hearts find no peace until they rest" in God (Saint Augustine 1961, 21). May sets a high standard for those who suffer from addiction and for those who do not: "we must not only accept and claim the sweetly painful incompleteness within ourselves, but also affirm it with all our hearts. Somehow we must come to fall in love with it" (May 1991, 181). When we do, as Christian pastors we will find that we have more in common with alcoholics and addicts than we thought. As one writer comments about another stigmatized group, "we'll realize that *they are us*" (Paris 2011, 110; italics hers).

Samuel M. Shoemaker, leader of the Oxford Group in America, prophetically remarks, "A.A. has derived its inspiration and impetus indirectly from the insights and beliefs of the church. Perhaps the time has come for the church to be reawakened and revitalized by the insights and practices found in A.A." (Alcoholics Anonymous World Services 1957, 270). Moreover, it is this writer's conclusion that the Twelve Step movement is a "church within the church," what has been referred to as *"ecclesiola in ecclesia"* (Hardin 1994a, 63; italics his). A member of Alcoholics Anonymous or other Twelve Step

Conclusion

group could well be what Jesuit theologian Karl Rahner calls an "anonymous Christian" (Rahner 1976, 283).[1]

---

1. According to Rahner, the "anonymous Christian" lives in God's "faith, hope, and love ... [but is] not yet a Christian at the social level (through baptism and membership of the Church)" (Rahner 1976, 283). Rahner's concept is anticipated by Dietrich Bonhoeffer's idea of "unconscious Christianity" (Bonhoeffer 2015, 475). As Geffrey B. Kelly observes, "Rahner's theory of the 'anonymous Christian' adds a theological coherence to what Bonhoeffer's ethical bearings had intuited" (Kelly 1995, 119).

Appendix A

Behavioral Manifestations and Complications of Addiction

1. Excessive use and/or engagement in addictive behaviors, at higher frequencies and/or quantities than the person intended, often associated with a persistent desire for and unsuccessful attempts at behavioral control.
2. Excessive time lost in substance use or recovering from the effects of substance use and/or engagement in addictive behaviors, with significant adverse impact on social and occupational functioning (e.g. the development of interpersonal relationship problems or the neglect of responsibilities at home, school, or work).
3. Continued use and/or engagement in addictive behaviors, despite the presence of persistent or recurrent physical or psychological problems which may have been caused or exacerbated by substance use and/or related addictive behaviors;
4. A narrowing of the behavioral repertoire focusing on rewards that are part of addiction; and
5. An apparent lack of ability and/or readiness to take consistent, ameliorative action despite recognition of problems.

(American Society of Addiction Medicine 2014, accessed May 1, 2014)

Appendix B

Alcohol Use Disorder Diagnostic Criteria

1. Alcohol is often taken in larger amounts or over a longer period than was intended.
2. There is a persistent desire or unsuccessful efforts to cut down or control alcohol use.
3. A great deal of time is spent in activities necessary to obtain alcohol, use alcohol, or recover from its effects.
4. Craving, or a strong desire or urge to use alcohol.
5. Recurrent alcohol use resulting in failure to fulfill major role obligations at work, school, or home.
6. Continued alcohol use despite having persistent or recurrent social or interpersonal problems caused or exacerbated by the effects of alcohol.
7. Important social, occupational, or recreational activities are given up or reduced because of alcohol use.
8. Recurrent alcohol use in situations in which it is physically hazardous.
9. Alcohol use is continued despite knowledge of having a persistent or recurrent physical or psychological problem that is likely to have been caused or exacerbated by alcohol.
10. Tolerance, as defined by either of the following:
    a. A need for markedly increased amounts of alcohol to achieve intoxication or desired effect.
    b. A markedly diminished effect with continued use of the same amount of alcohol.
11. Withdrawal, as manifested by either of the following:

Alcohol Use Disorder Diagnostic Criteria

    a. The characteristic withdrawal syndrome for alcohol. . . .
    b. Alcohol (or a closely related substance, such as a benzodiazepine) is taken to relieve or avoid withdrawal symptoms.

Mild: Presence of 2–3 symptoms.
Moderate: Presence of 4–5 symptoms.
Severe: Presence of 6 or more symptoms.

(American Psychiatric Association 2013, 490–1)

Appendix C

Gambling Disorder Diagnostic Criteria

1. Needs to gamble with increasing amounts of money in order to achieve the desired excitement.
2. Is restless or irritable when attempting to cut down or stop gambling.
3. Has made repeated unsuccessful efforts to control, cut back, or stop gambling.
4. Is often preoccupied with gambling. . . .
5. Often gambles when feeling distressed (e.g., helpless, guilty, anxious, depressed).
6. After losing money gambling, often returns another day to get even ("chasing" one's losses).
7. Lies to conceal the extent of involvement with gambling.
8. Has jeopardized or lost a significant relationship, job, or educational or career opportunity because of gambling.
9. Relies on others to provide money to relieve desperate financial situations caused by gambling.

Mild: 4–5 criteria met.
Moderate: 6–7 criteria met.
Severe: 8–9 criteria met.

(American Psychiatric Association 2013, 585–6)

Appendix D

Questionnaire Including Statement of Informed Consent

THE RESEARCH IN WHICH you are about to participate is designed to investigate views and attitudes of clergy toward the Twelve Step approach to addiction recovery (found in such groups as Alcoholics Anonymous, Al-Anon, Narcotics Anonymous, etc.). Herbert Hudson, a student in a DMin program at TEDS at Trinity International University, is conducting this project.

Please be assured that any information you provide will be held in strict confidence, and your anonymity will be respected at all times. At no time will your name be reported along with your responses. Please understand that your participation in this research is totally voluntary and you are free to withdraw from the study at any time. By your completion of this questionnaire, you are giving informed consent for the use of your responses in this research project.

Please note that in this questionnaire "Twelve Step Groups" refers to organizations such as the following: Alcoholics Anonymous, Narcotics Anonymous, and Al-Anon. "Christ-centered Twelve Step Groups" refers to biblically based programs such as Celebrate Recovery, Overcomers Outreach, and Alcoholics Victorious.

This survey will take approximately 10–15 minutes to complete. There is space on the bottom and backside of the last page to share additional thoughts on the subject.

After filling out this questionnaire, you may elect to participate in an individual interview at a future date.

APPENDIX D

QUESTIONNAIRE

Background

1. My religious denomination is: _____
2. It is my belief that the Florida Keys is more susceptible to an addictive life style than many other parts of the country. ❏ Yes ❏ No ❏ Don't know
3. I have attended a Twelve Step meeting. ❏ Yes ❏ No
4. In the past, my church has provided space for Twelve Step meetings. ❏ Yes ❏ No
5. At present, my church provides space for Twelve Step meetings. ❏ Yes ❏ No
6. There are members of my church who have active addictions. ❏ Yes ❏ No
7. There are members of my church who attend Twelve Step groups. ❏ Yes ❏ No
8. I encourage members of my church with active addictions to attend Twelve Step programs. ❏ Yes ❏ No

To What Extent Do You Agree or Disagree with the Following Statements:

9. "I am familiar with the subject of addiction and recovery in general."

❏	❏	❏	❏	❏
Strongly Agree	Somewhat Agree	Neutral No Opinion	Somewhat Disagree	Strongly Disagree

10. "I believe addiction is one of the most significant social problems of our time."

❏	❏	❏	❏	❏
Strongly Agree	Somewhat Agree	Neutral No Opinion	Somewhat Disagree	Strongly Disagree

11. "I think addiction is a disease, not a sin."

❏	❏	❏	❏	❏
Strongly Agree	Somewhat Agree	Neutral No Opinion	Somewhat Disagree	Strongly Disagree

Questionnaire Including Statement of Informed Consent

12. "I am familiar with Twelve Step programs such as A.A. and N.A."

    ☐ Strongly Agree   ☐ Somewhat Agree   ☐ Neutral No Opinion   ☐ Somewhat Disagree   ☐ Strongly Disagree

13. "My attitude toward Twelve Step programs is favorable."

    ☐ Strongly Agree   ☐ Somewhat Agree   ☐ Neutral No Opinion   ☐ Somewhat Disagree   ☐ Strongly Disagree

14. "I think that Twelve Step programs are based upon Christianity."

    ☐ Strongly Agree   ☐ Somewhat Agree   ☐ Neutral No Opinion   ☐ Somewhat Disagree   ☐ Strongly Disagree

15. "I am familiar with Christ-centered Twelve Step programs such as Celebrate Recovery and Overcomers Anonymous."

    ☐ Strongly Agree   ☐ Somewhat Agree   ☐ Neutral No Opinion   ☐ Somewhat Disagree   ☐ Strongly Disagree

16. "My attitude toward Christ-centered Twelve Step programs is favorable."

    ☐ Strongly Agree   ☐ Somewhat Agree   ☐ Neutral No Opinion   ☐ Somewhat Disagree   ☐ Strongly Disagree

17. "I think that people who are recovering from addiction can lead Christian lives."

    ☐ Strongly Agree   ☐ Somewhat Agree   ☐ Neutral No Opinion   ☐ Somewhat Disagree   ☐ Strongly Disagree

18. "I think that people who have recovered or are recovering from addiction should be welcomed in the church community."

    ☐ Strongly Agree   ☐ Somewhat Agree   ☐ Neutral No Opinion   ☐ Somewhat Disagree   ☐ Strongly Disagree

Appendix D

Other Questions

19. Your age: ❏ 18–25 ❏ 26–30 ❏ 31–40 ❏ 41–50 ❏ 51–60 ❏ 61+
20. Your gender: ❏ Male ❏ Female
21. Do you now work as a minister? ❏ Yes ❏ No
22. Did you graduate from a seminary? ❏ Yes ❏ No
23. Besides seminary, do you have other post-graduate education in social sciences? ❏ Yes ❏ No
24. Is there a history of addiction in your family? ❏ Yes ❏ No
25. What do you think is an appropriate response or recommendation to a parishioner experiencing addiction? (Check as many as may apply).
    - ❏ Do not Interfere
    - ❏ Terminate or Suspend Church Membership
    - ❏ Counseling
    - ❏ Prayer
    - ❏ Refer to Physician
    - ❏ Residential Rehabilitation
    - ❏ Christ-centered Residential Rehabilitation
    - ❏ Twelve Step Groups
    - ❏ Christ-centered Twelve Step Groups

Other Comments

Please feel free to write additional comments on your experience and feelings about addiction and Twelve Step groups below and on the reverse side of this page:

Questionnaire Including Statement of Informed Consent

26. I am willing to participate further by being interviewed on this topic:

Name: _____ Phone: _____

(Please include name and phone *if you would like to participate in an interview*. If you do not wish to participate in an interview, *do not give your name and phone*.)

Appendix E

Informed Consent Statement for Interview

THIS INTERVIEW WILL LAST approximately 60–75 minutes. The interviewer will take notes, and the interview will be audio recorded. The interviewer will destroy the interview recordings after the project is completed.

The research in which you are about to participate is designed to investigate views and attitudes of clergy toward the Twelve Step approach to addiction recovery (found in groups such as Alcoholics Anonymous, Narcotics Anonymous, Celebrate Recovery, etc.). Herbert Hudson, a student in a DMin program at TEDS at Trinity International University, is conducting this project. In this research, there are a series of questions; some of them may be similar to the survey you have recently taken.

Please be assured that any information you provide in this interview will be held in strict confidence and your anonymity will be respected at all times. At no time will your name be reported along with your responses. Please understand also that your participation in this interview is totally voluntary and you are free to withdraw at any time during the research.

"I acknowledge that I have been informed of, and understand, the nature and purpose of this interview, and I freely consent to participate."

Print Name: _____

Signed: _____ Date: _____

Appendix F

Interview Questions

1. What is your denomination?
2. What seminary training do you have?
3. Are you an ordained minister?
4. Which church do you presently serve?
   - How long have you been at this church?
   - How many members does this church have?
5. Which church did you serve previously?
   - How long were you there?
6. Is your ministry full-time?
   - If not, what other job do you have?
7. What percentage of members of your church would you say have active addictions?
   - What percentage of members of your church would you estimate attend Twelve Step meetings?
8. Have you visited Twelve Step meetings as a visitor or observer?
   - If so, would you describe your experience?
   - What is your opinion of and attitude toward Twelve Step groups?
9. Do you think Twelve Step groups are consistent with Christian principles, or do you feel that they depart from Christian beliefs?
   - In what ways you feel this?

Appendix F

10. Do you think Twelve Step groups are effective in dealing with addiction?
11. Do you think Twelve Step groups are effective in restoring people to serve Christ?
12. Does the church you serve provide meeting space for Twelve Step groups?
13. Are you familiar with Christ-centered Twelve Step groups such as Celebrate Recovery, Overcomers Outreach, or Alcoholics Victorious?
    - If so, do you favor Christ-centered groups over other Twelve Step programs?
14. How familiar are you with the subject of addiction and its treatment?
15. How did you gain this familiarity?
    - Through formal course work?
    - Self-study?
    - Internships or on-the-job experience?
16. Would you comment on how significant you feel the problem of addiction is in:
    - Your church?
    - Your community?
    - Your country?
17. Some say addiction is a sin; others say it is a disease.
    - What do you think?
    - Why do you feel this way?
18. Can people who have recovered from addiction be good Christians and good church members?
    - If so, what contributes to positive outcomes?
19. If a member of your congregation comes to you for counseling on addiction, what would be your guidance or advice to them?
20. Can God use addiction recovery to glorify him?

Appendix G

Outline of the Syllabus

I.   Educational Objectives. As a result of completing this course, participants will:
- A. Be aware of preconditions that influence views on and susceptibility to addiction
- B. Develop a knowledge base of current thinking on addictionology
- C. Become informed about the history and background of the Twelve Steps
- D. Become familiar with how the Twelve Step programs work; in particular, Alcoholics Anonymous and Celebrate Recovery
- E. Understand the spiritual features of the Twelve Step design and its relationship to Christianity

II.   Course Content Areas:
- A. Preconditions that influence views on and susceptibility to addiction
  1. The genetics of addiction
  2. History of addiction in families—designing a genogram
- B. Current thinking on addictionology
  1. Addiction as a social and cultural problem
  2. Addiction as a neurobiological disorder
  3. Addiction as a syndrome or spectrum disorder
     a. Alcohol and other drugs
     b. Process or behavior addictions
  4. Major characteristics of addiction
     a. Loss of will power and control
     b. Denial

APPENDIX G

        c. Tolerance
        d. Withdrawal
        e. Substitution/Reformation

Sources: Ries et al., *The ASAM Principles of Addiction Medicine;* American Psychiatric Association, *Diagnostic and Statistical Manual of Mental Disorders (DSM-5)*

  C. History and background of the Twelve Step movement

    1. Temperance and Prohibition

    2. The Oxford Group and Christian origins of A.A.

    3. Co-founders of A.A.

        a. Bill Wilson

        b. Dr. Bob Smith

    4. Literature of A.A.

        a. The *Big Book*

        b. *The Twelve Steps and Twelve Traditions*

Sources: William White, *Slaying the Dragon; Alcoholics Anonymous Comes of Age*

  D. How Twelve Step programs work

    1. The basics of A.A.

        a. The Twelve Steps

        b. The Twelve Traditions

    2. The essentials of Celebrate Recovery

        a. The Twelve Steps and Scripture Comparisons

        b. The Eight Principles based on the Sermon on the Mount

    3. Visitation at open A.A. and C.R. meetings

        a. Observations

        b. Reports

Sources: *Alcoholics Anonymous;The Twelve Steps and Twelve Traditions;* John Baker, *Celebrate Recovery*

  E. The spiritual features of the Twelve Step design and its relationship to Christianity

Outline of the Syllabus

1. Twelve Steps based upon Christianity?
   a. Is addiction a disease or a sin?
   b. Higher Power and the concept of God
   c. The character of Christ (i.e. in Celebrate Recovery)
   d. The role of prayer and miracles
   e. Fellowship as spiritual community
2. Twelve Steps depart from Christianity?

Sources: Ernest Kurtz, *Not-God;* Linda Mercadante, *Victims & Sinners;* Gerald May, *Addiction and Grace*

3. Specific roles for clergy
   a. Sponsorship and Fifth Step ministry as spiritual mentoring
   b. Counseling and referral
   c. Preaching effectively on addiction recovery and the Twelve Steps
   d. Allocating meeting space for Twelve Step Groups
   e. Facilitating Christ-centered Twelve Step Groups

Sources: Gregory Gabriel, "How Do You Hear a Fifth Step;" Mark Latcovich, "The Clergyperson and the Fifth Step;" John Baker with Rick Warren, *Celebrate Recovery*

III. Assignments:
   A. Pre-course paper on students' views toward addiction, including a genogram; the phenomena and social problems of addiction. Assigned length: 8–10 pages (30 percent of grade).
   B. Post-course paper on history and background of the Twelve Steps, how they work, the spiritual features of the Twelve Step design, and its relationship to Christianity. Assigned length: 18–20 pages (60 percent of grade).
   C. Class participation, including visitation reports (10 percent of grade).

Appendix G

IV. Course Bibliography

Alcoholics Anonymous World Services. 1957. *Alcoholics Anonymous Comes of Age: A Brief History of A.A.* New York: Alcoholics Anonymous World Services, Inc.

———. 2001. *Alcoholics Anonymous: The Story of How Many Thousands of Men and Women Have Recovered from Alcoholism.* 4th ed. New York: Alcoholics Anonymous World Services, Inc.

———. 2011. *Twelve Steps and Twelve Traditions.* New York: Alcoholics Anonymous World Services, Inc.

American Psychiatric Association. 2013. *Diagnostic and Statistical Manual of Mental Disorders (DSM-5).* 5th ed. Arlington, VA: American Psychiatric Association.

Baker, John. 2012a. *Celebrate Recovery: Stepping Out of Denial into God's Grace.* Grand Rapids, MI: Zondervan.

———. 2012b. *Celebrate Recovery: Taking an Honest and Spiritual Inventory.* Grand Rapids, MI: Zondervan.

———. 2012c. *Celebrate Recovery: Getting Right with God, Yourself, and Others.* Grand Rapids, MI: Zondervan.

———. 2012d. *Celebrate Recovery: Growing in Christ while Helping Others.* Grand Rapids, MI: Zondervan.

Gabriel, Gregory P. 1993. "How Do You Hear a Fifth Step?" *Journal of Ministry in Addiction & Recovery* 1, no. 1 (October): 41–46.

Kurtz, Ernest. 1991. *Not-God: A History of Alcoholics Anonymous.* Center City, MN: Hazelden.

Latcovich, Mark A. 1995. "The Clergyperson and the Fifth Step." *Journal of Ministry in Addiction and Chemical Dependency Treatment* 5, no. 2:79–89.

May, Gerald G. 1991. *Addiction & Grace: Love and Spirituality in the Healing of Addictions.* New York: Harper Collins.

Mercadante, Linda A. 1996. *Victims & Sinners: Spiritual Roots of Addiction and Recovery.* Louisville, KY: Westminster John Knox.

Ries, Richard K., David A. Fiellin, Shannon C. Miller, and Richard Saitz, eds. 2014. *The ASAM Principles of Addiction Medicine.* 5th ed. China: Wolters Kluwer.

White, William L. 2014. *Slaying the Dragon: The History of Addiction Treatment and Recovery in America.* 2nd ed. Bloomington, IL: Chestnut Health.

Bibliography

AA Grapevine. 2013. "Preamble." http://www.aa.org/assets/en_US/smf-92_en.pdf (accessed February 7, 2016).

"Addiction and the Family: A Seminary Curriculum." 2012. Kensington, MD: NACA. http://www.hacsalum.com/addiction-family-curriculum/ (accessed August 30, 2016).

Addiction411. 2014. http://www.addiction411.com/addiction-family-disease/ (accessed May 1, 2015).

Ahlstrom, Sydney E. 1972. *A Religious History of the American People*. New Haven: Yale University.

Albers, Robert H. 1994. "Spirituality and Surrender: A Theological Analysis of Tiebout's Theory for Ministry to the Alcoholic." *Journal of Ministry in Addiction & Recovery* 1, no. 2 (September) 47–69.

———. 1997. "Transformation: The Key to Recovery." *Journal of Ministry in Addiction & Recovery* 4, no. 1 (January) 23–36.

———. 1999. "The Spirit and Spirituality of Twelve Step Groups." *Journal of Ministry in Addiction & Recovery* 6, no. 1 (April) 1–7.

———. 2012. *Addiction and the Family: A Seminary Curriculum*. Kensington, MD: NACA.

Alcoholics Anonymous World Services. 1950. *Alcoholics Anonymous: The Story of How Many Thousands of Men and Women Have Recovered from Alcoholism*. 1st ed. New York: Alcoholics Anonymous World Services, Inc.

———. 1955. *Alcoholics Anonymous: The Story of How Many Thousands of Men and Women Have Recovered from Alcoholism*. 2nd ed. New York: Alcoholics Anonymous World Services, Inc.

———. 1957. *Alcoholics Anonymous Comes of Age: A Brief History of A.A.* New York: Alcoholics Anonymous World Services, Inc.

———. 1967. *The A.A. Way of Life: . . .Selected Writings of A.A.'s Co-Founder*. New York: Alcoholics Anonymous World Services, Inc.

———. 1975a. *Co-Founders of Alcoholics Anonymous: Biographical Sketches, Their Last Major Talks*. New York: Alcoholics Anonymous World Services, Inc.

———. 1975b. *Living Sober*. New York: Alcoholics Anonymous World Services, Inc.

Bibliography

———. 1976. *Alcoholics Anonymous: The Story of How Many Thousands of Men and Women Have Recovered from Alcoholism*. 3th ed. New York: Alcoholics Anonymous World Services, Inc.

———. 1980. *Dr. Bob and the Good Oldtimers: A Biography with Recollections of Early A.A. in the Midwest*. New York: Alcoholics Anonymous World Services, Inc.

———. 1984. *"Pass It On:" The Story of Bill Wilson and How the A.A. Message Reached the World*. New York: Alcoholics Anonymous World Services, Inc.

———. 1990. *Daily Reflections: A Book of Reflections by A.A. Members for A.A. Members*. New York: Alcoholics Anonymous World Services, Inc.

———. 2001. *Alcoholics Anonymous: The Story of How Many Thousands of Men and Women Have Recovered from Alcoholism*. 4th ed. New York: Alcoholics Anonymous World Services, Inc.

———. 2011. *Twelve Steps and Twelve Traditions*. New York: Alcoholics Anonymous World Services, Inc.

———. 2014. "Membership Survey." New York: Alcoholics Anonymous World Services, Inc. https://www.google.com/url?sa=t&rct=j&q=&esrc=s&source=web&cd=1&cad=rja&uact=8&ved=0ahUKEwi_s_qY_pvPAhXFMSYKHbxSABsQFghDMAA&url=http%3A%2F%2Fwww.aa.org%2Fassets%2Fen_US%2Fp-48_membershipsurvey.pdf&usg=AFQjCNE16Q-OchSWS33bliMs3yuUZ_FNPw (accessed September 19, 2016).

———. 2016. "Guidelines for Use of A.A.W.S. Copyrighted Material." http://www.aa.org/pages/en_US/content-use-policy (accessed December 5, 2016).

Alexander, Michelle. 2012. *The New Jim Crow: Mass Incarceration in the Age of Colorblindness*. New York: New Press.

American Psychiatric Association. 2013. *Diagnostic and Statistical Manual of Mental Disorders (DSM-5)*. 5th ed. Arlington, VA: American Psychiatric Association.

American Society of Addiction Medicine. 2005. "Public Policy Statement on the Definition of Alcoholism." http://www.asam.org/docs/publicy-policy-statements/1definition-of-alcoholism-2-902.pdf?sfvrsn=0 (accessed January 14, 2016).

———. 2014. "Definition of Addiction." http://www.asam.org/for-the-public/definition-of-addiction (accessed May 1, 2015).

Anonymous Press. 1992. *The Anonymous Press Mini Edition of Alcoholics Anonymous*. Malo, WA: Anonymous Press.

Apthorp, Stephen P. 1985. *Alcohol and Substance Abuse: A Clergy Handbook*. Wilton, CT: Morehouse Barlow.

Augustine. 1961. *Confessions*. Translated by R. S. Pine-Coffin. New York: Penguin.

B., Dick. 1997. *The Good Book and the Big Book: A.A.'s Roots in the Bible*. Kihei, HI: Paradise Research.

———. 2005. *The James Club and the Original A.A. Program's Absolute Essentials*. Kihei, HI: Paradise Research.

B., Dick, and Ken B. 2012. *Stick with the Winners! How to Conduct More Effective 12-Step Recovery Meetings Using Conference-Approved Literature*. Kihei, HI: Paradise Research.

Bailey, Carol A. 2007. *A Guide to Qualitative Field Research*. 2nd ed. Thousand Oaks, CA: Pine Forge.

Baker, John. 2012a. *Celebrate Recovery: Stepping Out of Denial into God's Grace*. Grand Rapids, MI: Zondervan.

Bibliography

———. 2012b. *Celebrate Recovery: Taking an Honest and Spiritual Inventory*. Grand Rapids, MI: Zondervan.

———. 2012c. *Celebrate Recovery: Getting Right with God, Yourself, and Others*. Grand Rapids, MI: Zondervan.

———. 2012d. *Celebrate Recovery: Growing in Christ While Helping Others*. Grand Rapids, MI: Zondervan.

Bickel, Warren K. and Marc N. Potenza. 2006. "The Forest and the Trees: Addiction as a Complex Self-Organizing System." In *Rethinking Substance Abuse: What the Science Shows, and What We Should Do About It*, edited by William R. Miller and Kathleen M. Carroll, 8–21. New York: Guilford.

Bobgan, Martin, and Deidre Bobgan. 1991. *12 Steps to Destruction: Codependency Recovery Heresies*. Santa Barbara, CA: Eastgate.

Bonhoeffer, Dietrich. 2015. *Letters and Papers from Prison*. Translated by Isabel Best. Minneapolis: Fortress.

The Book that Started It All: The Original Working Manuscript of Alcoholics Anonymous. 2010. Center City, MN: Hazelden.

Burns, Bob, Tasha D. Chapman, and Donald C. Guthrie. 2013. *Resilient Ministry: What Pastors Told Us About Surviving and Thriving*. Downers Grove, IL: Intervarsity.

C., Dave. 2000. "A Fresh Big Book, a Pen, and Some Paper." *AA Grapevine* 57, no. 1 (June) 9–11.

Calahan, Don, and Robin Room. 1974. *Problem Drinking Among American Men*. New Haven, CT: College & University.

Carnes, Patrick J. 1991. *Don't Call It Love: Recovery From Sexual Addiction*. New York: Bantam.

———. 2001. *Out of the Shadows: Understanding Sexual Addiction*. 3rd ed. Center City, MN: Hazelden.

Celebrate Recovery. 2015a. "Celebrate Recovery 12 Steps and Biblical Comparisons." http://www.celebraterecovery.com/index.php/about-us/twelve-steps (accessed July 12, 2017).

———. 2015b. "Celebrate Recovery's Eight Recovery Principles." http://www.celebraterecovery.com/index.php/about-us/2015-11-25-05-17-36 (accessed July 12, 2017).

Cheever, Susan. 2004. *My Name is Bill: Bill Wilson—His Life and the Creation of Alcoholics Anonymous*. New York: Washington Square.

Chester, Tim, and Steve Timmis. 2008. *Total Church: A Radical Reshaping Around Gospel and Community*. Wheaton, IL: Crossway.

Chestnut, Glenn F. 2006. *Changed By Grace: V.C. Kitchen, the Oxford Group, and A.A.* New York: iUniverse.

Childress, Anna Rose. 2006. "What Can Human Brain Imaging Tell Us about Vulnerability to Addiction and to Relapse?" In *Rethinking Substance Abuse: What the Science Shows, and What We Should Do About It*, edited by William R. Miller and Kathleen M. Carroll, 46–60. New York: Guilford.

Claytor, Robert M. 1998. "Recovery as Quest for Spiritual Transformation." *Journal of Ministry in Addiction & Recovery* 5, no. 1 (January) 31–36.

Clinebell, Howard J., Jr. 1956a. "The Emmanuel Movement." http://silkworth.net/emmanuel_movement/01003.htm (accessed May 4, 2015).

———. 1956b. *Understanding and Counseling the Alcoholic: Through Religion and Psychology*. New York: Abingdon.

Bibliography

———. 1968. *Understanding and Counseling the Alcoholic: Through Religion and Psychology.* Revised and Enlarged Edition. Nashville: Abingdon.

———. 1998. *Understanding and Counseling Persons with Alcohol, Drug, and Behavioral Addictions.* Nashville: Abingdon.

Conley, Paul C., and Andrew A. Sorensen. 1971. *The Staggering Steeple: The Story of Alcoholism and the Churches.* Philadelphia: Pilgrim.

Cook, Christopher C. H. 2006. *Alcohol, Addiction and Christian Ethics.* Cambridge: Cambridge University Press.

Crawford, Robin. 1997. "The Presbyterian Church in the United States of America." *Journal of Ministry in Addiction & Recovery* 4, no. 2: 69–79.

Creswell, John W. 2014. *Research Design: Qualitative, Quantitative, and Mixed Methods Approaches.* 4th ed. Los Angeles: Sage.

Dann, Bucky. 2002. *Addiction: Pastoral Responses.* Nashville: Abingdon.

Dubiel, Richard M. 1999. "Paul Tillich: Key Philosophical Theologian of the Mid-Twentieth Century." http://hindsfoot.org/dubtill.html (accessed December 29, 2015).

———. 2004. *The Road to Fellowship: The Role of the Emmanuel Movement and the Jacoby Club in the Development of Alcoholics Anonymous.* Lincoln, NE: iUniverse.

Dunningham, Kent. 2011. *Addiction and Virtue: Beyond the Models of Disease and Choice.* Downers Grove, IL: IVP Academic.

Erickson, Millard J. 2013. *Christian Theology.* Grand Rapids, MI: Baker.

Fingarette, Herbert. 1988. *Heavy Drinking: The Myth of Alcoholism as a Disease.* Berkeley: University of California.

Finley, James R. 2004. *Integrating the 12 Steps into Addiction Therapy: A Resource Collection and Guide for Promoting Recovery.* New York: Wiley.

Fitzgerald, Robert. 1995. *The Soul of Sponsorship: The Friendship of Fr. Ed Dowling, S.J. and Bill Wilson in Letters.* Center City, MN: Hazelden.

Flores, Philip J. 2004. *Addiction as an Attachment Disorder.* New York: Jason Aronson.

Fosdick, Harry Emerson. 1956. *The Living of These Days: An Autobiography.* New York: Harper.

Foster, Richard J. 1992. *Prayer: Finding the Heart's True Home.* San Francisco: HarperCollins.

———. 2008. *Celebration of Discipline: The Path to Spiritual Growth.* London: Hodder & Stoughton.

Fowler, James W. 1993. "Alcoholics Anonymous and Faith Development." In *Research on Alcoholics Anonymous: Opportunities and Alternatives,* edited by Barbara S. McCrady and William R. Miller, 113–35. New Brunswick, NJ: Rutgers Center of Alcohol Studies.

Gabriel, Gregory P. 1994. "How Do You Get the Spiritual Part of the Program?" *Journal of Ministry in Addiction & Recovery* 1, no. 1 (October) 41–46.

———. 1995. "How Do You Hear a Fifth Step?" *Journal of Ministry in Addiction & Recovery* 2, no. 2 (September) 97–115.

Gagnon, Robert A. J. 2001. *The Bible and Homosexual Practice: Texts and Hermeneutics.* Nashville: Abingdon.

Gore, Josh. 2015. "Study: Keys Outdrink Other Florida Counties." *Florida Keys Free Press.* http://keysnews.com/node/66440 (accessed Febrary 6, 2016).

Bibliography

Green Acres Baptist Church. n.d. "History of Celebrate Recovery." http://www.celebraterecoverygabc.com/History-of-Celebrate-Recovery.html (accessed September 17, 2016).

Greggs, Tom. 2011. *Theology Against Religion: Constructive Dialogues with Bonhoeffer and Barth*. New York: T&T Clark.

Grudem, Wayne. 1994. *Systematic Theology: An Introduction to Biblical Doctrine*. Grand Rapids, MI: Zondervan.

H., Terry. 1994. "Francis." *AA Grapevine* 51, no. 5 (October) 6–7.

Hardin, Michael. 1994a. "The Twelve Step Program and Christian Spirituality." *Journal of Ministry in Addiction & Recovery* 1, no. 1 (October) 47–68.

———. 1994b. "Let God Be God: A Theological Justification for the Anonymity of God in the 12 Step Program." *Journal of Ministry in Addiction & Recovery* 1, no. 2 (September) 9–22.

Hart, Kenneth E. 1999. "A Spiritual Interpretation of the 12-Steps of Alcoholics Anonymous: From Resentment to Forgiveness to Love." *Journal of Ministry in Addiction & Recovery* 6, no. 2 (September) 25–39.

Hartigan, Francis. 2000. *Bill W.: A Biography of Alcoholics Anonymous Cofounder Bill Wilson*. New York: St. Martins.

Harvard Medical School. 2011. "How Addiction Hijacks the Brain." *Harvard Mental Health Letter* 28, no. 1 (July) 1–3.

Hopson, Ronald E., and M. Jay Moses. 1996. "Theology of Paradox: A Pauline Contribution to the Understanding and Treatment of Addictions." *Journal of Ministry in Addiction & Recovery* 3, no. 1 (January) 7–15.

Howard, Peter. 1961. *Frank Buchman's Secret*. Garden City, NY: Doubleday.

Hudson, Herbert E., IV. 2016a. "Developing a Syllabus for Pastors and Those in Ministerial Training on Addiction Recovery Through Twelve Step Philosophy." DMin diss., Trinity Evangelical and Divinity School. Proquest (10257687).

———. 2016b. "Outline of the Syllabus: Christianity and Addiction Recovery Through Twelve Step Philosophy." http://www.terryhudson.com/addictionrecoverysyllabus.pdf (accessed November 5, 2016).

Humphreys, Keith, and Elizabeth Gifford. 2006. "Religion, Spirituality, and the Troublesome Use of Substances." In *Rethinking Substance Abuse: What the Science Shows, and What We Should Do About It*, edited by William R. Miller and Kathleen M. Carroll, 257–74. New York: Guilford.

Hunter, W. Bingham. 1986. *The God Who Hears*. Downers Grove, IL: Intervarsity.

Huxley, Aldous. 1932. *Brave New World*. New York: Harper.

Jellinek, E. Morton. 1960. *The Disease Concept of Alcoholism*. New Haven, CT: Hillhouse.

John of the Cross. 2003. *Dark Night of the Soul*. Translated by E. Allison Peers. Mineola, NY: Dover.

Kapsch, Sharon G. 1997. "A Lutheran Reflection of the 'Twelve Steps of AA.'" *Journal of Ministry in Addiction & Recovery* 4, no. 2 (September) 53–67.

Keil, C. F., and Franz Delitzsch. 2006. Vol. 1, *Commentary on the Old Testament: The Pentateuch*. Peabody, MA: Hendrickson.

Keller, John E. 1966. *Ministering to Alcoholics*. Minneapolis: Augsburg.

Kelly, Geffrey B. 1995. "'Unconscious Christianity' and the 'Anonymous Christian' in the Theology of Dietrich Bonhoeffer and Karl Rahner." *Philosophy and Theology* 9, no. ½: 117–49.

Bibliography

Knippel, Charles T. 1994. *The 12 Steps: The Church's Challenge and Opportunity.* St. Louis: Concordia.

Koob, George F. 2006. "Neurobiology of Addiction: A Hedonic Calvinist View." In *Rethinking Substance Abuse: What the Science Shows, and What We Should Do About It,* edited by William R. Miller and Kathleen M. Carroll, 25–45. New York: Guilford.

Kurtz, Ernest. 1987. "Alcoholics Anonymous: A Phenomenon in American Religious History." In *Religion and Philosophy in the U.S.A.,* vol. 2, edited by Peter Freese, 447–62. Essen, Germany: Verlag Die Blaue Eule. http://silkworth.net/religion_clergy/01081.html (accessed December 21, 2015).

———. 1991. *Not-God: A History of Alcoholics Anonymous.* Center City, MN: Hazelden.

———. 1999. *The Collected Ernie Kurtz.* Wheeling, WV: Bishop of Books.

———. 2002. "Alcoholics Anonymous and the Disease Concept of Alcoholism." http://www.williamwhitepapers.com/pr/Dr.%20Ernie%20Kurtz%20on%20AA%20%26%20the%20Disease%20Concept,%202002.pdf (accessed August 23, 2016).

———. 2008a. *The Collected Ernie Kurtz.* New York: Author's Choice.

———. 2008b. "Why A.A. Works: The Intellectual Significance of Alcoholics Anonymous." In *The Collected Ernie Kurtz,* 177–228. Bloomington, IN: iUniverse. http://hindsfoot.org/tcek11.pdf (accessed April 6, 2016).

Kurtz, Ernest, and Katherine Ketcham. 1992. *The Spirituality of Imperfection: Storytelling and the Search for Meaning.* New York: Bantam.

Kurtz, Ernest, and William White. 2003. "Alcoholics Anonymous." In *Alcohol and Temperance in Modern History,* edited by Jack S. Blocker, David M. Fahey, and Ian R. Tyrrell, 27–31. Santa Barbara, CA: ABC-CLIO. https://books.google.com/books?id=BuzNzm-xol8C&pg=PR23&dq=alcohol+and+temperance+in+modern+society&hl=en&sa=X&ved=0CDAQ6AEwAGoVChMIzd7tkZXaxgIVorYeChocLAjN#v=onepage&q=alcohol%20and%20temperance%20in%20modern%20society&f=false (accessed July 14, 2015).

Latcovich, Mark A. 1995. "The Clergyperson and the Fifth Step." *Journal of Chemical Dependency Treatment* 5, no. 2: 79–89. https://www.google.com/url?sa=t&rct=j&q=&esrc=s&source=web&cd=1&ved=0ahUKEwjqgOrli6vOAhVLFx4KHcC2BRgQFggeMAA&url=http%3A%2F%2Fwww.nacoa.org%2Fpdfs%2FLatcovich-The%2520Clergyperson%2520and%2520the%2520Fifth%2520Step.doc.pdf&usg=AFQjCNEAhi7cWDjC1DJtlu_WSTx8drzEpg&cad=rja (accessed August 5, 2016).

Lattimore, Vergel. 1997. "The Theology of Addiction: Spiritual, Psychological, and Social Roots." *Journal of Ministry in Addiction & Recovery* 4, no. 1 (January) 47–62.

Lean, Garth. 1988. *On the Tail of a Comet: The Life of Frank Buchman.* Colorado Springs: Helmers & Howard.

Lee, Gary K. 1996. "The Beatitudes of Jesus and the 12 Steps of AA." *Journal of Ministry in Addiction & Recovery* 3, no. 1 (January) 17–32.

Lende, Daniel. 2010. "Addiction & Learning: More than Glutamate and Dopamine." http://blogs.plos.org/neuroanthropology/2010/09/14/addiction-learning-more-than-glutamate-and-dopamine/ (accessed January 17, 2016).

Madsen, William. 1974. *The American Alcoholic: The Nature-Nurture Controversy in Alcoholic Research and Therapy.* Springfield, IL: Charles C. Thomas.

Mann, Marty. 1981. *New Primer on Alcoholism: How People Drink, How to Recognize Alcoholics, and What to Do About Them.* New York: Holt, Rinehart, and Winston.

Bibliography

Matto, Michele S. 1991. *The 12 Steps in the Bible: A Path to Wholeness for Adult Children.* New York: Paulist.

May, Gerald G. 1991. *Addiction & Grace: Love and Spirituality in the Healing of Addictions.* New York: Harper Collins.

McCarthy, Katherine. 1984. "The Emmanuel Movement and Richard Peabody." *Journal of Studies on Alcohol* 45, no. 1: 59–74. http://silkworth.net/emmanuel_movement/01001.htm (accessed December 29, 2015).

McCormick, Patrick T. 1989. *Sin as Addiction.* New York: Paulist.

McCrady, Barbara S., and William R. Miller, eds. 1993. *Research on Alcoholics Anonymous: Opportunities and Alternatives.* New Brunswick, NJ: Rutgers Center of Alcohol Studies.

McDonough, William. 2012. "Sin and Addiction: Alcoholics Anonymous and the Soul of Christian Sin-Talk." *Journal of the Society of Christian Ethics* 32, no. 1: 39–55. http://www.jstor.org/stable/23562887 (accessed February 7, 2016).

Means, Patrick A. 2006. *Men's Secret Wars.* Grand Rapids, MI: Revell.

Mercadante, Linda A. 1994. "Sin, Addiction, and Freedom." In *Reconstructing Christian Theology*, edited by Rebecca S. Chopp and Mark Lewis Taylor, 220–44. Minneapolis: Augsburg Fortress.

———. 1996a. *Victims & Sinners: Spiritual Roots of Addiction and Recovery.* Louisville: Westminster John Knox.

———. 1996b. "Addiction." In *Dictionary of Feminist Theologies*, edited by Letty M. Russell and J. Shannon Clarkson, 3. Louisville: Westminster John Knox.

———. 1997. "Sin, Gender, and Addiction." *Journal of Ministry in Addiction & Recovery* 4, no. 1 (January) 37–45.

———. 1998. "Addiction and Recovery." *Christian Century* 115, no. 9 (March 18–25) 302–314.

———. 2005. "The Church and Addiction Recovery." *Christian Networks Journal* (Summer) 50–56.

———. 2007. "Pelagian Theology Lives On in Science." *Vital Theology* 4, no. 4 (November) 4–5.

———. 2009. "The Religious and Theological Roots of Alcoholics Anonymous." In *Praeger International Collection on Addictions: Faces of Addiction, Then and Now*, vol. 1, edited by Angela Browne-Miller, 95–105. Westport, CT: Praeger.

———. 2010. "Helping Addicts Move Beyond the Spiritual Wading Pool: A New Approach to Religion and Spirituality in the Healing of Addictions." *International Journal of Existential Psychology & Psychotherapy* 3, no. 1 (January) 1–6.

Mertens, Donna M. 2009. *Transformative Research and Evaluation.* New York: Guilford.

Michael, Katherine S. 1998. "The Twelve Steps: A Biblical Foundation for Recovery." *Journal of Ministry in Addiction & Recovery* 5, no. 2 (September) 75–84.

Miller, J. Keith. 1991. *A Hunger for Healing: The Twelve Steps as a Classic Model for Christian Spiritual Growth.* San Francisco: Harper Collins.

Miller, William R. 1993. "Toward a Biblical Perspective on Drug Use." *Journal of Ministry in Addiction & Recovery* 2, no. 2 (September) 77–85.

———. 2006. "Motivational Factors in Addictive Behavior." In *Rethinking Substance Abuse: What the Science Shows, and What We Should Do About It*, edited by William R. Miller and Kathleen M. Carroll, 134–50. New York: Guilford.

———. 2010. *Integrating Spirituality into Treatment: Resources for Practitioners.* Washington DC: American Psychological Association.

Bibliography

Miller, William R., and Ernest Kurtz. 1994. "Models of Alcoholism Used in Treatment: Contrasting AA and Other Perspectives With Which It is Often Confused." *Journal of Studies on Alcohol* 55, no. 2 (March) 159–66. https://www.google.com/url?sa=t&rct=j&q=&esrc=s&source=web&cd=1&ved=0ahUKEwiC58D29P_LAhXEQCYKHcJZBfYQFgg8MAA&url=http%3A%2F%2Fwww.williamwhitepapers.com%2Fpr%2FDrs.%2520Miller%2520%2526%2520Kurtz%25200n%2520Models%25200f%2520Alcoholism%2C%25201994.pdf&usg=AFQjCNFFgfIzLcntBoETh5ixFzGmE6tj3A&cad=rja (accessed April 8, 2016).

Miller, William R., and Kathleen M. Carroll, eds. 2006. *Rethinking Substance Abuse: What the Science Shows, and What We Should Do About It*. New York: Guilford.

Miller, William R., and Stephen Rollnick. 2013. *Motivational Interviewing: Helping People Change*. 3rd ed. New York: Guilford.

Morgan, Oliver J., and Merle Jordon, eds. 1999. *Addiction and Spirituality: A Multidisciplinary Approach*. St. Louis: Chalice.

Morreim, Dennis C. 1990. *The Road to Recovery: Bridges Between the Bible and the Twelve Steps*. Minneapolis: Augsburg.

Myers, J. B. 2007. *Faith and Addiction: A Faith Alternative to the Twelve Steps Theory and Disease Model of Addiction Treatment*. Lexington, KY: n.p.

National Association for Children of Alcoholics. n.d. "Clergy Certificate Program." http://nocoa.org/clergy.htm (accessed May 18, 2015).

National Association for Children of Alcoholics, Johnson Institute, and Substance Abuse and Mental Health Services Administration. 2003. "Substance Abuse and the Family: Defining the Role of the Faith Community Clergy Training and Curriculum Development." http://www.samhsa.gov/sites/default/files/competency.pdf (accessed February 8, 2016).

National Center on Addiction and Substance Abuse at Columbia University. 2001. "So Help Me God: Substance Abuse, Religion and Spirituality." New York: Author House. https://www.google.com/url?sa=t&rct=j&q=&esrc=s&source=web&cd=2&cad=rja&uact=8&ved=0ahUKEwi5zOajotLKAhVB2B4KHckIAGgQFggkMAE&url=http%3A%2F%2Fwww.casacolumbia.org%2Fdownload%2Ffile%2Ffid%2F1198&usg=AFQjCNGg2Wnq1XTmeFUKqOb_u7v1hEOTIA (accessed January 30, 2016).

Nelson, James B. 2004. *Thirst: God and the Alcoholic Experience*. Louisville: Westminster John Knox.

O'Neil, Mike S. 1998. *Power to Choose: Twelve Steps to Wholeness*. Antioch, TN: Sonlight.

Orange, A. 2013. "The Religious Roots of Alcoholics Anonymous and the Twelve Steps." http://www.orange-papers.org/orange-rroot030.html (accessed May 1, 2015).

Paris, Jenell Williams. 2011. *The End of Sexual Identity*. Downers Grove, IL: Intervarsity.

Parsec, Mark. 2011. "A Biblical Perspective of Addiction and Recovery: Theology of Recovery." http://www.searchwarp.com/swa226012.htm (accessed May 1, 2015).

Peabody, Richard R. 1930. *The Common Sense of Drinking*. Ventura, CA: Binghamus.

Peck, M. Scott. 2003. *The Road Less Travelled: A New Psychology of Love, Traditional Values, and Spiritual Growth*. New York: Simon & Schuster.

———. 2013. Interview by David Sheff. http://www.davidsheff.com/article/m-scott-peck/ (accessed September 29, 2014).

Peele, Stanton. 1995. *Diseasing of America: How We Allowed Recovery Zealots and the Treatment Industry to Convince Us That We Are Out of Control*. San Francisco: Jossey-Bass.

Bibliography

Peterson, Anna L. 2009. *Everyday Ethics and Social Change: The Education of Desire.* New York: Columbia University.
Piper, John. 1997. *A Hunger for God: Desiring God Through Fasting and Prayer.* Wheaton, IL: Crossway.
Pittman, Bill, and Dick B. 1994. *Courage to Change: The Christian Roots of the Twelve-Step Movement.* Center City, MN: Hazelden.
Plantinga, Cornelius, Jr. 1995. *Not the Way It's Supposed to Be: A Breviary of Sin.* Grand Rapids: William B. Eardmans.
Playfair, William L. 1991. *The Useful Lie.* Wheaton, IL: Crossway.
Pollan, Michael. 2001. *The Botany of Desire: A Plant's Eye View of the World.* New York: Random House.
Rahner, Karl. 1976. *Ecclesiology, Questions in the Church, the Church in the World.* Vol. XIV, Theological Investigations. Translated by David Bourke. New York: Seabury.
Ries, Richard K., David A. Fiellin, Shannon C. Miller, and Richard Saitz, eds. 2014. *The ASAM Principles of Addiction Medicine.* 5th ed. China: Wolters Kluwer.
Robinson, Bryan E. 2014. *Chained to the Desk.* New York: New York University.
Room, Robin. 1993. "Alcoholics Anonymous as a Social Movement." In *Research on Alcoholics Anonymous: Opportunities and Alternatives,* edited by Barbara S. McCrady and William R. Miller, 167–87. New Brunswick, NJ: Rutgers Center of Alcohol Studies. http://www.robinroom.net/alcoanon.htm (accessed July 13, 2015).
Roper, Anita. 1966. *The Anonymous Christian.* Translated by Joseph Donceel. New York: Sheed and Ward.
Royce, James E. 1985. "Sin or Solace? Religious Views on Alcohol and Alcoholism." *Journal of Drug Issues* 15, no. 1 (Winter) 51–61.
Rush, Benjamin. 2011. *An Inquiry Into the Effects of Ardent Spirits Upon the Human Body and Mind: With an Account of the Means of Preventing, and of the Remedies for Curing Them.* Charleston, SC: Nabu. (Orig. pub. 1785).
Ryan, T.C. 2012. *Ashamed No More: A Pastor's Journey Through Sex Addiction.* Downers Grove, IL: Intervarsity.
Ryken, Philip G. 2003. *City On a Hill: Reforming the Biblical Pattern for the Church in the 21st Century.* Chicago: Moody.
Sandoz, Charles J. 1999a. "Exploring the Spiritual Experience of the Twelve Steps of Alcoholics Anonymous." *Journal of Ministry in Addiction & Recovery* 6, no. 1 (April) 99–107.
———. 1999b. "The Spiritual Experience in Recovery: A Closer Look." *Journal of Ministry in Addiction & Recovery* 6, no. 2 (September) 53–59.
Sasser, John E. 2007. "F. C. Oetinger and the Serenity Prayer." http://ourspecial.net/misc/sereneoetinger.htm (accessed October 30, 2015).
Schneider Institute for Health Policy. 2001. "Substance Abuse: The Nation's Number One Health Problem." http://www.google.com/url?sa=t&rct=j&q=&esrc=s&source=web&cd=2&ved=0CC4QFjAB&url=http%3A%2F%2Fwww.rwjf.org%2Fcontent%2Fdam%2Ffarm%2Freports%2Freports%2F2001%2Frwjf13550&ei=2Kg7VZjfEe3hsASgy4CoDA&usg=AFQjCNGkb7IYqehho8moT8aB-9JJR4sw1g&bvm=bv.91665533,d.cWc (accessed May 1, 2015).
Selby, Saul. 2000. *Twelve Step Christianity: The Christian Roots and Application of the Twelve Steps.* Center City, MN: Hazelden.

Bibliography

Shaffer, Howard J. 2012. "Defining Addiction, Making Research Transparent, and Dealing With the DSM-V." http://addiction-dirkh.blogspot.com/2012/01/interview-with-howard-shaffer-director.html (accessed January 5, 2016).

Shaffer, Howard J., et al. 2004. "Toward a Syndrome Model of Addiction: Multiple Expressions, Common Etiology." *Harvard Review of Psychiatry* 12, no. 6 (Nov–Dec) 367–74. doi: 10.1080/10673220490905705

Sheff, David. 2013. *Clean: Overcoming Addiction and Ending America's Greatest Tragedy.* New York: Houghton Mifflin Harcourt.

Shoemaker, Helen Smith. 1967. *I Stand By the Door: The Life of Sam Shoemaker.* Waco, TX: Word.

Shoemaker, Samuel M. n.d. *What the Church Has to Learn From Alcoholics Anonymous.* Baltimore: Diocese of Maryland, Diocesan Committee on Alcoholism. http://www.a-1associates.com/aa/LETTERS%20ETC/WhatChurches.htm (accessed April 19, 2016).

———. 2008. *The Conversion of the Church: The Genius of Fellowship.* N.p.: Tuchy Palmieri.

Simmons, David L. 2012. *Christianity and Alcoholics Anonymous: Competing or Compatible?* Bloomington, IN: WestBow.

Stark, Paul R. 2004. "Celebrate Recovery: A Review." http://www.google.com/url?sa=t&rct=j&q=&esrc=s&source=web&cd=1&ved=0CCoQFjAA&url=http%3A%2F%2Fprovisionhouse.org%2FCelebrateRecoveryReview.pdf&ei=O55DVeqmNefIsQTHyIDwBQ&usg=AFQjCNEiiZT-eDmiWlnBGLJioqwYkPEqvQ&bvm=bv.92189499,d.cWc (accessed May 1, 2015).

———. 2010. "Alcoholics Anonymous and the Church: A History Misunderstood." http://www.scribd.com/doc/42973762/Alcoholics-Anonymous-and-the-Church (accessed May 1, 2015).

Swanson, Liz, and Teresa McBean. 2011. *Bridges to Grace: Innovative Approaches to Recovery Ministry.* Grand Rapids, MI: Zondervan.

Thompson, James W. 2006. *Pastoral Ministry According to Paul.* Grand Rapids, MI: Baker.

Thomsen, Robert. 1975. *Bill W.* New York: Harper and Row.

Tillich, Paul. 1955. *The Shaking of the Foundations.* New York: Charles Scribner's & Sons.

———. 1967. *Systematic Theology.* 3 vols. New York: Harper & Row.

Tzschentke, T. M. and W. J. Schmidt. 2003. "Glutamatergic Mechanisms in Addiction." *Molecular Psychiatry* 8, no. 4: 373–82. http://www.nature.com/mp/journal/v8/n4/full/4001269a.html (accessed January 18, 2016). doi:10.1038/sj.mp.4001269

United States Census. 2015. http://www.quickfacts.census.gov/qfd/states/12/12087.html (accessed May 1, 2015).

Van Gelder, Craig. 2000. *The Essence of the Church: A Community Created By the Spirit.* Grand Rapids, MI: Baker.

Van Yperen, Jim. 2002. *Making Peace: A Guide to Overcoming Church Conflict.* Chicago: Moody.

Volkow, Nora D. and Kenneth R. Warren. 2014. "Drug Addiction: The Neurobiology of Behavior Gone Awry." In *The ASAM Principles of Addiction Medicine,* 5th ed., edited by Richard K. Ries, David A. Fiellin, Shannon C. Miller, and Richard Saitz, 3–18. China: Wolters Kluwer.

Vyhmeister, Nancy J. 2008. *Quality Research Papers: For Students of Religion and Theology.* 2nd ed. Grand Rapids, MI: Zondervan.

Bibliography

Walker, Richmond. 2013. *Twenty-Four Hours a Day.* Center City, MN: Hazelden.
Welch, Edward T. 2001. *Addictions: A Banquet in the Grave.* Phillipsburg, NJ: P&R.
———. 2003. "Developing a Theology of Drug Abuse." *Journal of Biblical Ethics in Medicine* 4, no. 4: 12–13. http://www.bmei.org/jbem/volume4/num4/welch_developing_a_theology_of_drug_abuse.php (accessed May 1, 2015).
White, William L. 1996. *Pathways From the Culture of Addiction to the Culture of Recovery.* Center City, MN: Hazelden.
———. 2001. "Pre-A.A. Alcoholic Mutual Aid Societies." *Alcoholism Treatment Quarterly* 19, no. 2 (May) 1–21.
———. 2003. "Alcoholic Mutual Aid Societies." In *Alcohol and Temperance in Modern History,* edited by Jack S. Blocker, David M. Fahey, and Ian R. Tyrrell, 24–27. Santa Barbara, CA: ABC-CLIO. http://www.williamwhitepapers.com/pr/2003AlcoholicMutualAidSocietiesinUS.pdf (accessed July 13, 2015).
———. 2014. *Slaying the Dragon: The History of Addiction Treatment and Recovery in America.* 2nd ed. Bloomington, IL: Chestnut Health.
White, William L., and Ernest Kurtz. 2008. "Twelve Defining Moments in the History of Alcoholics Anonymous." In *Recent Developments in Alcoholism,* edited by Marc Galanter and Lee Ann Kaskutas, vol 18. Totawa, NJ: Humana. http://www.google.com/url?sa=t&rct=j&q=&esrc=s&source=web&cd=1&ved=0CB4QFjAAahUKEwikneKsvNjGAhUFiwoKHQfgAuE&url=http%3A%2F%2Fwww.williamwhitepapers.com%2Fpr%2F2008TwelveDefiningMomentsinAAHistory.pdf&ei=y9-jVeSLJYWWNofAi4gO&usg=AFQjCNEFjzk7ShBqa6HQYAGK-S3N6qoA4w&bvm=bv.97653015,d.eXY (accessed July 13, 2015).
Wilson, Bill. 1953. "The Original Six Steps of A.A." http://www.thejaywalker.com/pages/sixstep.html (accessed September 7, 2016).
———. 2011. *The Language of the Heart.* New York: AA Grapevine.
Wilson, Lois. 1979. *Lois Remembers.* New York: Al-Anon Family Group.
Wing, Nell. 2009. "Origin of the Serenity Prayer: A Historical Paper." http://www.aa.org/assets/en_US/smf-129_en.pdf (accessed December 23, 2015).
"Women Clergy: A Growing and Diverse Community." 2015. http://www.religionlink.com/source-guides/women-clergy-a-growing-and-diverse-community/ (accessed September 22, 2016).
Woodruff, C. Roy. 2003. "Role of the Clergy: The Effects of Alcohol and Drugs on the Person and the Family." *Seminary Journal* 9 (Winter) 8–13. http://scholar.google.com/scholar_url?url=http://www.nacoa.org/pdfs/Woodruff%2520%2520Sem%2520Dept%25209-5-06.pdf&hl=en&sa=X&scisig=AAGBfm1_R4xFBvDdDhAM_o8GcprkYZTSLQ&nossl=1&oi=scholarr (accessed December 20, 2015).
Woolverton, John F. 1983. "Evangelical Protestantism and Alcoholism 1933–1962: Episcopalian Samuel Shoemaker, the Oxford Group and Alcoholics Anonymous." *Historical Magazine of the Protestantism Episcopal Church* 52 (March) 153–65. http://www.silkworth.net/religion_clergy/01079.html (accessed December 21, 2015).
Wuthnow, Robert. 1996. *Sharing the Journey: Support Groups and America's New Quest for Community.* New York: Free Press.
Z., John. 2012. *Grace in Addiction: The Good News of Alcoholics Anonymous for Everybody.* Charlottesville, VA: Mockingbird.

www.ingramcontent.com/pod-product-compliance
Lightning Source LLC
Chambersburg PA
CBHW071504150426
43191CB00009B/1413